2010

AP CHEMISTRY
CRASH COURSE

By Michael D'Alessio
Watchung Hills Regional High School
Warren, New Jersey

D1025649

Research & Education Association
Visit our website at: www.rea.com

Research & Education Association
61 Ethel Road West
Piscataway, New Jersey 08854
E-mail: info@rea.com

AP CHEMISTRY CRASH COURSE

Printed in the United States of America

Library of Congress Control Number 2010940980

ISBN-13: 978-0-7386-0697-2
ISBN-10: 0-7386-0697-9

AP CHEMISTRY CRASH COURSE TABLE of CONTENTS

PART V

Descriptive Chemistry

PART VI

Laboratory and Chemical Calculations

ABOUT THIS BOOK

REA's *AP Chemistry Crash Course* is the first book of its kind for the last-minute studier or any AP student who wants a quick refresher on the course. The *Crash Course* is based on a careful analysis of the AP Chemistry Course Description outline and actual AP test questions.

Written by an AP teacher, our easy-to-read format gives students a crash course in Chemistry. The targeted review chapters are grouped by topics, offering you a concise way to learn all the important facts, formulas, and terms before exam day.

Unlike other test preps, REA's *AP Chemistry Crash Course* gives you a review specifically focused on what you really need to study in order to ace the exam. The introduction discusses the keys for success and shows you strategies to help you build your overall point score.

Parts Two through Six are a complete crash course in Chemistry. These 32 chapters focus on the subjects tested on the AP exam and cover everything from the Structure of Matter to Laboratory and Chemical Calculations.

The remaining chapters focus exclusively on the AP Chemistry exam format. The author discusses major AP Chemistry themes and their relationship to the test, and also includes a chapter on the free-response portion of the exam.

No matter how or when you prepare for the AP Chemistry exam, REA's *Crash Course* will show you how to study efficiently and strategically, so you can boost your score!

To check your test readiness for the AP Chemistry exam, either before or after studying this *Crash Course*, take our **FREE online practice exam**. To access your free practice exam, *visit www.rea.com/crashcourse* and follow the on-screen instructions. This true-to-format test features automatic scoring of the multiple-choice questions, detailed explanations of all answers, and will help you identify your strengths and weaknesses so you'll be ready on exam day!

Good luck on your AP Chemistry exam!

ABOUT OUR AUTHOR

Michael D'Alessio earned his B.S. in Biology from Seton Hall University and his M.S. in Biomedical Sciences from the University of Medicine and Dentistry of New Jersey. In 2004, he earned his Executive Master of Arts in Educational Leadership from Seton Hall University.

Mr. D'Alessio has had an extensive career teaching all levels of mathematics and science, including AP Chemistry, as well as biology, physics, algebra, geometry, calculus and statistics. In 2003, Mr. D'Alessio received the Governor's Teacher of the Year recognition for his classroom work at Watchung Hills Regional High School. In 2004, Mr. D'Alessio received a Certificate of Recognition of Excellence in Science Teaching from Sigma Xi, the Scientific Research Society of Rutgers University and in 2005, he was voted National Honor Society Teacher of the Year by the students of Watchung Hills.

Currently, Mr. D'Alessio serves as the Supervisor of the Mathematics and Business Department at Watchung Hills Regional High School in Warren, New Jersey, overseeing a department of 30 teachers. He also participates in numerous SAT workshops around the country, preparing students for the mathematics portion of the test.

ACKNOWLEDGMENTS

In addition to our author, we would like to thank Larry B. Kling, Vice President, Editorial, for his overall guidance, which brought this publication to completion; Pam Weston, Publisher, for setting the quality standards for production integrity and managing the publication to completion; Diane Goldschmidt, Senior Editor, for editorial project management; Alice Leonard, Senior Editor, for preflight editorial review; Rachel DiMatteo, Graphic Artist, for page designs, and Weymouth Design, for designing our cover.

We also extend our special thanks to Rebekah Warner and Karyn O'Neill for technically reviewing the manuscript and Kathy Caratozzolo of Caragraphics, for typesetting this edition.

PART I:

INTRODUCTION

Keys for Success on the AP Chemistry Exam

AP Chemistry textbooks are very thick and contain thousands of facts and concepts. If the AP Chemistry exam contained all these facts, the challenge to earn a good score on the exam would be daunting. Studying for this exam requires the student to be a pragmatic learner who can delineate the important tested material from the material that is "interesting to know."

This book will help you become more pragmatic in your studying and streamline your chances of scoring a 4 or 5 on this exam. The keys to success on the exam include knowing the following:

1. **The Content of the Advanced Placement Chemistry Examination**

   The Advanced Placement Chemistry curriculum is based on the content of an introductory chemistry course taught at the college level. The topics taught in the class reflect major topics that are presented in a number of college level textbooks. The curriculum of the course also includes thematic-based laboratories and chemical calculations. In order to succeed on the exam, students need to master the basic concepts of chemistry and apply these concepts to various situations in a traditional test format. The make-up of the exam is based on the following percentages in five topics of understanding:

   I.   Structure of Matter, 20%

   II.   States of Matter, 20%

   III. Reactions, 35–40%

   IV.   Descriptive Chemistry, 10–15%

   V.   Laboratory, 5–10%

The AP Chemistry examination is 3 hours and 5 minutes in length and consists of a 90 minute multiple-choice question section and a 95 minute free-response question section. There are 75 multiple-choice questions and 6 free-response questions.

Section I.   75 multiple-choice questions (90 minutes)—50% of the grade

The number of multiple-choice questions from each topic is based on the percentages above. On this section of the exam NO CALCULATOR is allowed.

Section II.   6 free-response question section (95 minutes)—50% of the grade

Part A (55 minutes): CALCULATOR ALLOWED

- Problem 1—Equilibrium Free Response Question (20% of Section II score)

- Problem 2—Unknown Topic (could be quantitative laboratory based, 20% of Section II score)

- Problem 3—Unknown Topic (could be quantitative laboratory based, 20% of Section II score)

Part B (40 minutes): NO CALCULATOR ALLOWED

- Problem 4—Reaction Question (3 reactions total, must answer all, 10% of Section II score)

- Problem 5—Unknown Topic (could be qualitative laboratory based, 15% of Section II score)

- Problem 6—Unknown Topic (could be qualitative laboratory based, 15% of Section II score)

2. The Multiple-Choice Questions

The multiple-choice questions are simply designed to test your ability to know and recall facts about a particular topic relating to basic chemistry concepts. For example:

When the chemical equation below is completed and balanced, what statement best represents the reaction?

$$.....C_5H_{12} (g) + ...O_2 (g) \boxed{?}$$

(A) 1 mole of pentane is consumed to 6 moles of water produced

(B) 1 mole of pentane is produced to 6 moles of water consumed

(C) 1 mole of pentane is consumed to 1 moles of water produced

(D) 1 mole of pentane is produced to 1 moles of water consumed

(E) 1 mole of pentane is consumed to 8 moles of oxygen produced

The correct answer is (A). The equation represents a combustion reaction that will produce carbon dioxide and water. When balanced the equation looks like the following:

$$C_5H_{12} (g) + 8O_2 (g) \rightarrow 5CO_2(g) + 6H_2O(g)$$

The good news is content-based questions make up a good portion of the AP exam. It is essential to know these basic ideas when confronted by this type of question. This book will give you the content you need to know in a *Crash Course* manner.

Non-calculation-based chemistry questions are also part of this section. Since no calculator is allowed, some multiple-choice questions will ask you to select the proper mathematical setup. For example:

At 25°C, 300 milliliters of an ideal gas exerts a pressure of 740 mm Hg. The volume of the gas at 0°C and 760 mm Hg is found from which of the following expression?

(A) $300 \times \dfrac{760}{740} \times \dfrac{273}{298}$ mL

(B) $300 \times \dfrac{740}{760} \times \dfrac{0}{25}$ mL

(C) $300 \times \dfrac{760}{740} \times \dfrac{25}{0}$ mL

(D) $300 \times \dfrac{760}{740} \times \dfrac{298}{273}$ mL

(E) $300 \times \dfrac{740}{760} \times \dfrac{273}{298}$ mL

The correct answer is (E). Using the combined gas law formula and plugging in values, the following mathematical setup is determined: $\dfrac{V_1 P_1}{T_1} = \dfrac{V_2 P_2}{T_2}$, $\dfrac{(740)(300)}{298} = \dfrac{(760)(V_2)}{273}$.

Solving for V_2 gives you $300 \times \dfrac{740}{760} \times \dfrac{273}{298}$ mL

Multiple-Choice Question Format

Type I. Traditional Multiple-Choice Questions with choices (A) through (E). There is only one correct answer! For example:

Atoms of element X have the same electron configuration shown below. The compound most likely formed with lithium, Li, is

$$1s^2 2s^2 2p^6 3s^2 3p^4$$

(A) LiX

(B) LiX_2

(C) Li_2X

(D) LiX_3

(E) Li_3X

The correct answer is (C). Lithium ion has +1. Element X has a −2 charge.

Type II. Heading Multiple-Choice-Questions with choices (A) through (E). There is only one correct answer for each question. However, the answers could be used in a set of questions only once, more than once, or not at all. These questions usually make up the first 15 questions of the multiple-choice section.

Questions 1–5

    (A) K

    (B) Al

    (C) Cl

    (D) Hg

    (E) Ba

1. This atom has two unpaired electrons

2. Is pale green and used in bleaches

3. Liquid metal at STP

4. Most abundant metal in the crust of the Earth

5. When freshly cut, it will tarnish immediately

Correct answers:

1. (E)   2. (C)   3. (D)   4. (B)   5. (A)

3. How is the test scored?

Section I. Scores on the multiple-choice section of the exam will be based on the number of questions answered correctly. Points are not deducted for incorrect answers and no points will be awarded for unanswered questions.

Multiple-Choice Raw Score

    Number Right = _____

Section II. The free-response section is scored by multiplying the number of raw points earned on each essay by a weighted conversion.

Free-Response Question 1 _____ × 1.50 = _____
(possible points out of 10)

Free-Response Question 2 _____ × 1.50 = _____
(possible points out of 10)

Free-Response Question 3 _____ × 1.50 = _____
(possible points out of 10)

Free-Response Question 4 _____ × 1.50 = _____
(possible points out of 10)

Free-Response Question 5 _____ × 1.50 = _____
(possible points out of 10)

Free-Response Question 6 _____ × 1.50 = _____
(possible points out of 10)

Combined Free-Response Score = _____

Composite Score =
MC Raw Score + Combined Free-Response Score

Composite Score Range*	AP Grade
85–150	5
65–84	4
45–64	3
30–44	2
0–29	1

* Composite Score Ranges Change Year to Year

On the low end, you can score 85 out of a possible 150 points (57%) and *still* earn a 5 on the test. To earn a 4 you need 65 points out of a possible 150 or 43%!!!! This *Crash Course* will help you achieve the highest grade possible on this test.

4. What is the breakdown of AP Chemistry grades across the country?

Year	% Students Earning Examination Grade of				
	5	4	3	2	1
2006	17.0%	18.4%	22.4%	17.7%	24.5%
2007	15.3%	18.0%	23.0%	18.5%	25.3%
2008	18.4%	17.5%	20.0%	14.3%	29.9%

Data obtained from College Board Student Grade Distribution Reports 2006–2008

The data above indicates that, in 2008, about one out of every five students who took the AP Chemistry examination earned a 5, while a staggering 29.9% of students earned a 1. In 2008, there were 101,000 AP Chemistry test takers, an all-time high. This *Crash Course* is tailored for all of the students represented in the data and will help you to earn a grade that will get you college credit for chemistry.

5. Using College Board and REA Materials to Supplement Your *Crash Course*

This *Crash Course* contains everything you need to know to score a 4 or a 5. You should, however, supplement it with materials provided by the College Board. The AP Chemistry Course Description Booklet, and the 1999, 2002, and 2008 released AP Chemistry Exams, can all be ordered from the College Board's Online Store at *http:// store.collegeboard.com*. (Note that the format of the AP Chemistry exam changed in 2007, and is not represented in these tests.) In addition, the College Board's AP Central website at *http://apcentral. collegeboard.com* contains a wealth of materials, including essay questions with exemplars and rubrics. And finally, REA's *AP Chemistry (10th Edition)* contains excellent narrative chapters that supplement this *Crash Course* material.

PART II:

STRUCTURE OF MATTER

Atomic Theory

I. Atomic Theory and Atomic Structure

A. Evidence for the atomic theory

1. *Law of the conservation of mass*—Mass is neither created nor destroyed in a chemical reaction. French chemist Antoine Lavoisier used quantitative experiments involving the combustion of oxygen to prove the law.

2. *Law of definite proportion*—A chemical compound always contains the same proportion of elements by mass. In H_2O the mass ratio of hydrogen to oxygen is always 1 to 8. French chemist Joseph Proust used quantitative experiments to prove the law.

3. *Law of multiple proportions*—When elements combine, they do so in a ratio of small whole numbers. For example, the mass of oxygen that will combine with 1 gram of carbon to form carbon monoxide is 1.33 grams. The mass of oxygen that combines with 1 gram of carbon to form carbon dioxide is 2.66. The masses are in ratio 2.66:1.33 = 2:1, a simple whole number ratio. English chemist John Dalton used quantitative experiments to prove the law.

4. *Dalton's Atomic Theory*
   i.   All matter is made up of atoms.
   ii. The atoms of a specific element are identical. Atoms of different elements are different.
   iii. Chemical compounds are formed by the combination of elements.
   iv. Atoms are re-organized in a chemical reaction.

5. *Cathode Ray Tube*
   i.   Performed by J.J. Thomson

    ii. Negatively charged particles were emitted from the cathode region of a cathode ray tube.

    iii. Charged particles were repelled by a negative field, indicating that the charge was negative and the particles were electrons.

    iv. Plum-pudding model or electrons being dispersed in pudding of positive charge was the leading model of the time for the atom.

6. *Millikan Experiment*

    i. Performed by American scientist Robert Millikan.

    ii. Experiment was based on adjusting voltage applied to charged oil droplets and measuring how much was necessary to keep the droplet from falling.

    iii. Used to determine the size of the charge of electrons.

7. *Rutherford Experiment—Gold Foil Experiment*

    i. Gold foil was bombarded with alpha particles.

    ii. Anticipated results were based on plum-pudding model: the alpha particles would travel through the atom with no deflections.

    iii. Actual results indicated that some of the alpha particles were deflected because of the concentrated center of positive particles (nucleus).

    iv. Plum-pudding model could not explain the structure of the atom, and therefore a nuclear model had to be true.

8. *Modern View of the Atom*

    i. Nucleus—contains protons (positive charge) and neutrons (neutral charge)

    ii. Nucleus is extremely small when compared to the size of the atom and is very dense. Accounts for the majority of the mass of the atom.

    iii. Electrons (negative charge) surround the nucleus and make up a majority of the space of an atom.

A. Atomic Masses

  1. Physical Means

    i. Modern Atomic Masses are based on ^{12}C (carbon twelve). ^{12}C = 12 atomic mass units (amu).

ii. *Mass Spectrometer*—device that bombards an atom with high speed electrons. The bombardment causes movement of electrons off the atom producing an ion that has a deflection pattern that is dependent on the mass of the ion. Ratio of masses of atoms are compared to ^{12}C and multiplied by 12 amu.

2. *Isotopes*—different atoms of the same element having a different number of neutrons.

3. The atomic masses of elements in the periodic table are dependent on the mixture of isotopes of the particular atom of interest. The atomic mass on the periodic table is the "weighted average" of the isotopes of the particular atom.

   i. Example Calculation

Isotope	Mass (amu)	Abundance	Calculation
^{24}Mg	23.98	78.99%	23.98(.7899) = 18.94
^{25}Mg	24.98	10.00%	24.98(.1000) = 2.498
^{26}Mg	25.98	11.01%	25.98(.1101) = 2.860
			24.30 amu

   ii. Sample AP Problem
   The atomic mass of element R is 75.16. If there are 2 naturally occurring isotopes of R called ^{75}R and ^{77}R, what is the natural abundance of each isotope?

   x = abundance of ^{75}R
   1 − x = abundance of ^{77}R

   $75x + 77(1 − x) = 75.16$
   $75x + 77 − 77x = 75.16$
   $−2x = −1.84$
   $x = 92\%$
   $^{75}R = 92\%, \ ^{77}R = 8\%$

B. Atomic Number and Mass Number; Isotopes

1. *Atomic Number*—number of protons found in an atom. Called "Z" for abbreviation purposes. Identifies an element.

2. *Mass Number*—number of protons and neutrons found in an atom. Called "A" for abbreviation purposes.

3. *Nuclear Symbol*

$^{A}_{Z}X$ A = mass number, Z = atomic number,
X = element symbol

$^{40}_{19}K$ (potassium forty has 19 protons, 21 neutrons, 19 electrons)

4. *Ions*—atoms or molecules in which the total number of electrons is not equal to the total number of protons

5. *Cation*—positively charged ion

$^{40}_{19}K^{1+}$ (19 protons, 21 neutrons, 18 electrons)

6. *Anion*—negatively charged ion

$^{33}_{16}S^{2-}$ (16 protons, 17 neutrons, 18 electrons)

C. Electron Energy Levels: Atomic Spectra, Quantum Numbers, Atomic Orbitals

1. *Atomic Spectrum of Hydrogen*—based on giving H_2 gas molecules a high-energy flash in which the H_2 molecules absorb energy breaking H-H bonds. The hydrogen atoms are *excited* energy-containing atoms. The excited atoms release energy in the form of light (energy = light) producing an emission spectrum that is unique to hydrogen. The emission spectrum is quantized or can be mathematically calculated by the formula: *Energy* = hv (h = Planck's constant 6.63×10^{-34} J s; v = frequency).

2. *Bohr Model of Hydrogen*—proposed the quantum model for hydrogen atom: electrons move in a circular orbit around the nucleus of an atom. Bohr proposed *energy levels* that were consistent with the atomic spectrum of hydrogen. When Bohr's Model was extrapolated to other atoms, it was found to have fundamental flaws.

3. *Quantum Mechanical Model of the Atom*—discovered by Heisenberg, de Broglie, and Schrodinger and based on quantum mechanics. The model is based on electrons having wave like properties and reside in *orbitals* or discrete areas based on a wave function where electrons reside. Each orbital can hold two electrons. The *Heisenberg Uncertainty Principle* states "that it is impossible to pinpoint the exact location and velocity of an electron."

4. *Quantum Numbers*—a series of numbers used to classify the location of an electron
    i.   *n, the Principal Quantum Number*
        1. Can be any whole number from 1 to infinity.
        2. Determines the energy level of the atom.
    ii. *l, the Angular Momentum Quantum Number*
        1. Each value of l corresponds to a different type of subshell.
        2. l can be no larger than n – 1.

Magnitude of l	Subshell	Number of Orbitals
0	s	1
1	p	3
2	d	5
3	f	7

   iii. m_l, *the Magnetic Quantum Number*
        1. Specifies which orbital within a subshell the electron is assigned to.
        2. Values of m_l range from –l to +l.

Principal Quantum Number	Angular Momentum Quantum Number	Magnetic Quantum Number	Orbitals in Subshell
1	0	0	One 1s
2	0	0	One 2s
	1	–1,0,1	Three 2p
3	0	0	One 3s
	1	–1,0,1	Three 3p
	2	-2,–1,0,1,2	Five 3d
4	0	0	One 4s
	1	–1,0,1	Three 4p
	2	–2,–1,0,1,2	Five 4d
	3	–3,–2,–1,0,1,2,3	Seven 4f

   iv. m_s, *the Spin Quantum Number*
        1. Specifies the angular momentum of the electron.
        2. Values of m_s are either +1/2 or –1/2.

Sample AP Question

One of the outermost electrons in a calcium atom in ground state can be represented by which sets of four quantum numbers?

(A)   4, 2, 0, 1/2

(B)   4, 1, 1, 1/2

(C)   4, 1, 0, 1/2

(D)   4, 0, 1, 1/2

(E)   4, 0, 0, 1/2

The correct answer is (E). Ca is in period 4 (n = 4), s orbital (l = 0), $m_l = 0$, $m_s = 1/2$

D. Writing Electron Configurations

1s		
2s		2p
3s		3p
4s	3d	4p
5s	4d	5p
6s	5d	6p
7s	6d	
	4f	
	5f	

s block—Group 1A and 2A
p block—Groups 3A through 8A
d block—transition metals
f block—lanthanides and actinides

1. *Electron Configuration*—a method to indicate the distribution of electrons in an atom.
2. Number indicates the energy level (i.e., $1s^2$ indicates 1st energy level).
3. Letter indicates the subshell (orbital): s, p, d, f.
4. Superscript indicates the number of electrons (i.e., $1s^2$ indicates 2 electrons).

5. Each orbital holds 2 electrons
   i.   s subshell contains 1 orbital, thus holding a maximum of 2 electrons
   ii. p subshell contains 3 orbital, thus holding a maximum of 6 electrons
   iii. d subshell contains 5 orbital, thus holding a maximum of 10 electrons
   iv. f subshell contains 7 orbital, thus holding a maximum of 14 electrons

6. *Aufbau (German for "building up") Principle*—electrons fill the lowest energy orbital first.

7. *Pauli Exclusion Principle*—in a given atom no two electrons can have the same set of four quantum numbers.

8. *Hund's Rule*—the lowest energy state (most stable) of an atom is the one having the maximum number of unpaired electrons.

9. *Orbital Diagram*—the use of boxes to represent the building up of electrons.

10. *Noble Gas Configuration (aka Abbreviated Electron Configuration)*—using the preceding noble gas to represent the core electrons of the atom. For example, $Ca = [Ar]4s^2$

11. *Valence Electrons*—the outermost electrons of an atom that determine the chemical properties of the atom.

12. *Electron Configuration of Ions*—outer electrons are removed or added first.
    i.   Na: $1s^2 2s^2 2p^6 3s^1 \rightarrow Na^{1+}: 1s^2 2s^2 2p^6 + e^-$
    ii. S: $1s^2 2s^2 2p^6 3s^2 3p^4 + 2e^- \rightarrow S^{2-}: 1s^2 2s^2 2p^6 3s^2 3p^6$

13. *Isoelectronic*—atoms having the same electron configurations.
    i. Mg^{2+} is isoelectronic with Ne
    ii. Te^{2-} is isoelectronic with Xe
    iii. N^{3-} is isoelectronic with Ne
    iv. Be^{2+} is isoelectronic with He

14. *Paramagnetism* is the property of attraction to a magnetic field. The atoms of paramagnetic substances contain unpaired electrons.

15. *Diamagnetism* is the property of repulsion by a magnetic field. Those of diamagnetic substance generally contain only paired electrons.

16. Examples

Element	Electron Configuration	Orbital Diagram
H	$1s^1$	1s [↑]
He	$1s^2$	1s [↑↓]
Li	$1s^22s^1$	1s [↑↓] 2s [↑]
Be	$1s^22s^2$	1s [↑↓] 2s [↑↓]
B	$1s^22s^22p^1$	1s [↑↓] 2s [↑↓] 2p [↑][ ][ ]
C	$1s^22s^22p^2$	1s [↑↓] 2s [↑↓] 2p [↑][↑][ ]
N	$1s^22s^22p^3$	1s [↑↓] 2s [↑↓] 2p [↑][↑][↑]

Example Problems

Write the electron configuration for the element phosphorus.
$1s^2 2s^2 2p^6 3s^2 3p^3$

Write the abbreviated electron configuration for Fe^{3+}.
$[Ar]3d^5$

E. Periodic Relationships: Atomic Radii, Ionization Energies, Electrons Affinities, Oxidation State

1. *Atomic Radii*—the distance from the atomic nucleus to the outermost electron shell. For main group elements (1A–8A), atomic radii increases down a group and decreases across a period. Down a group, the radius gets larger because more electrons are added to the outer shells of the atom. Across a period adds more protons and electrons to the atom, but the effective nuclear charge is greater attracting electrons to the nucleus and thus decreasing the atomic radius.

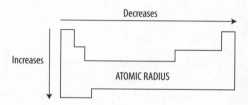

2. *Ionization Energy (IE)*—the energy required to remove an electron from an atom in gas phase

$$Ca\ (g) \rightarrow Ca^+(g) + e^-\ IE_1 = \ \ \ 590\ kJ/mol$$
$$Ca^+\ (g) \rightarrow Ca^{2+}(g) + e^-\ IE_2 = \ 1145\ kJ/mol$$
$$Ca^{2+}\ (g) \rightarrow Ca^{3+}(g) + e^-\ IE_3 = \ 4912\ kJ/mol$$

Removing an electron(s) from an atom increases the attractive force between the protons and the remaining electrons. The ionization energy becomes extremely high when the ion formed has a stable octet such as Ca^{2+}. For main block elements, the ionization energy trend increases across a period and up a group. Across a period adds more protons, increasing the effective nuclear charge and making the "pull" on the electrons greater. Going up a group decreases the size of the atom and makes it harder to pull an electron away, thus a higher ionization energy.

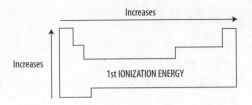

Sample AP Question

Based on the chart below element X is in which periodic group?

Ionization Energies for Element X (kJ/mol)				
First	Second	Third	Fourth	Fifth
540	1651	2650	14921	17345

    (A)   Group 1A

    (B)   Group 2A

    (C)   Group 3A

    (D)   Group 4A

    (E)   Group 5A

The correct answer is (C), Group 3A. Since the largest energy group is from third to fourth, element X must achieve noble gas configuration after losing 3 electrons.

3. *Electron Affinity (EA)*—ability of an atom to acquire an electron

$$F(g) + e^- \rightarrow F^-(g) \qquad EA = -590 \text{ kJ/mol}$$

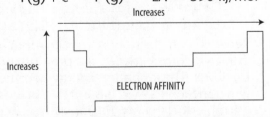

The sign for electron affinity can be tricky to interpret. When an electron is accepted by an atom, it is an exothermic process, therefore energy is released, and the sign for the energy is negative. There is an increase across a period and up a group. This indicates that energy is released upon the addition of an electron.

4. *Electronegativity*—the ability of an atom to attract shared electrons towards itself

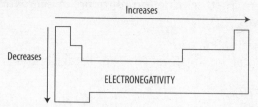

Electronegativity increases across a period and decreases going down a group. Since the nucleus has a positive charge it will pull on the valence electrons resulting in smaller atoms having high electronegativity values.

E. Ionic Radii

1. Cations are generally smaller since they have lost outer electrons.
2. Anions are generally larger since they have gained outer electrons.

F. Oxidation States (Numbers)

1. *Oxidation State*—charge that an atom has when either in a molecule or ion.
2. Oxidation numbers are used to determine oxidizing and reducing agents in redox reactions.
3. Rules for Assigning Oxidation Numbers
   i.   Any atom in its pure form has an oxidation number of 0. Examples include Cl_2, Fe, S_8.
   ii. For monatomic ions, the oxidation number is equal to the charge. Examples include +2 for Ba, −1 for Br, and −2 for S.
   iii. The oxidation number of H is +1 when combined with a nonmetal and −1 when combined with a metal.
   iv. The oxidation number of O is −2.
   v.   Cl, Br, and I are always −1, except when paired with oxygen and fluorine.
   vi. The sum of the oxidation numbers of a neutral compound must be zero. The sum of the oxidation numbers in a polyatomic must be equal to its charge.

Sample AP Question

Determine the oxidation numbers of each atom in the following:

A. Fe_2S_3

$S = -2$, $Fe = +3$

Total $S = -6$, Total $Fe = +6$, Total Charge $= 0$

B. $Cr_2O_7^{2-}$

$O = -2$, $Cr = +6$

Total $O = -14$, Total $Cr = +12$, Total Charge $= -2$

G. Properties of Elements

1. Group 1A—Alkali Metals (Li, Na, K, Rb, Cs, Fr)
   i. Most chemically reactive of all metals
   ii. Rapidly oxidize
   iii. Does not include hydrogen, which is not a metal
   iv. Increase in density down the group
   v. Soft to the touch
   vi. Decrease in melting and boiling point down the group
   vii. Lose 1 valence electron to become stable (noble gas configuration), therefore have a +1 charge
   viii. React with non-metals to form ionic compounds
2. Group 2A—Alkaline Earth Metals (Be, Mg, Ca, Sr, Ba, Ra)
   i. React with water to form basic solutions or hydroxides
   ii. Higher melting and boiling points compared to Group 1A
   iii. Higher density compared to Group 1A
   iv. Harder to the touch compared to Group 1A
   v. Lose 2 valence electrons to become stable (noble gas configuration), therefore have a +2 charge.
3. Group 3A—The Boron Group (B, Al, Ga, In, Tl)
   i. Increased metallic character down the group; B is the only non-metal.
   ii. Lose 3 valence electrons to become stable (noble gas configuration), therefore have a +3 charge.
   iii. Most important element in group is aluminum.
      1. Most abundant metal on earth
      2. Used as structural material

4. Group 4A—The Carbon Group (C, Si, Ge, Sn, Pb)
   i.   Increased metallic character down the group; C (non-metal), Si and Ge (metalloids)
   ii. All group 4A elements can form 4 covalent bonds to nonmetal (CH_4, $SiBr_4$), and have tetrahedral geometry
   iii. Can have a valence number of +2, +4, or –4
   iv. Tin (Sn^{2+}, Sn^{4+}) common ions
   v.   Lead (Pb^{2+}, Pb^{4+}) common ions

5. Group 5A—The Nitrogen Group (N, P, As, Sb, Bi)
   i.   Only one metal (Bi), N, P (non-metals), As, Sb (metalloids)
   ii. Nitrogen makes up about 78% of earth's atmosphere
   iii. Gain 3 valence electrons to become stable (noble gas configuration), therefore have a –3 charge.

6. Group 6A—Chalcogens (O, S, Se, Te, Po)
   i.   O, S, Se are all non-metals; Te and Po are metalloids
   ii. Oxygen makes up 21% of atmosphere
   iii. Sulfur is foul smelling; thiols are sulfur containing organic compounds
   iv. Gain 2 valence electrons to become stable (noble gas configuration), therefore have a –2 charge

7. Group 7A—Halogens or salt formers (F, Cl, Br, I, At)
   i.   All exist as diatomic molecules, except At
   ii. All non-metals
   iii. Combine with Group 1A to form ionic salts
   iv. Gain 1 valence electron to become stable (noble gas configuration), therefore have a –1 charge.

8. Group 8A—Noble Gases (He, Ne, Ar, Kr, Xe, Rn)
   i.   Least reactive of all elements; inert gases
   ii. All non-metals
   iii. Have a full outer shell of 8 electrons therefore are stable

9. Transition Metals—The B elements
   i.   *d*-block elements
   ii. Have multiple oxidations states and produce various colors
   iii. Very hard
   iv. High melting and boiling points

10. Lanthanides and Actinides
    i. *f*-block elements
    ii. Rare earth metals

I. Key Concepts of Periodic Table
    1. Metals
        i. Most elements on periodic table
        ii. Conduction of heat and electricity
        iii. Malleable or able to be hammered into a thin sheet
        iv. Ductile or can be drawn into a wire
        v. Lustrous or shiny
    2. Nonmetals
        i. Lack all the physical properties of metals
        ii. Brittle or fall apart
    3. Metalloids or semi-metals
        i. Have intermediate properties of metals and nonmetals

Chemical Bonding

I. Binding Forces

A. Valence Electrons

1. The outermost shell of electrons in any atom determines the valence of that atom.
2. Core electrons—the remaining electrons that are not involved in bonding

B. Lewis Symbols for Atoms

1. Valence electrons can be represented by the use of dots placed around the symbol of the atom.
2. Valence number = group number
3. Octet of electrons is formed when 4 pairs of electrons are around the atom.

Group 1A ns^1	Group 2A ns^2	Group 3A ns^2np^1	Group 4A ns^2np^2	Group 5A ns^2np^3	Group 6A ns^2np^4	Group 7A ns^2np^5	Group 8A ns^2np^6
Li •	• Be •	• Ḃ •	• Ċ •	• Ṅ •	Ö •	Ċl •	Ne

C. Ionic Bonding

1. Ionic bonds are formed when one or more valence electrons are transferred between atoms.
2. Group 1A and 2A atoms have very low ionization energies, therefore valence electrons are easily removed from their outer subshell. As a result, alkali and alkaline earth metals form cations with a noble gas configuration.

3. Group 6A and 7A atoms have high electron affinities and form anions by adding electrons to their outer shell.
4. Ionic Compounds
   i. Generally a metal and nonmetal pair
   ii. Solids
   iii. No electrical conductivity when solid, but when aqueous, highly conductive (ionic compound dissociates)
   iv. High melting and boiling point
   v. Arranged in a 3-dimensional lattice/crystal structure
   vi. *Lattice Energy*—measurement of the energy of formation of one mole of a crystalline ionic compound.

D. Covalent Bonding

1. Covalent bonds are formed when electron pairs are shared amongst atoms.
2. Generally a nonmetal and nonmetal pair.
3. Lewis Structure—representation of a covalent molecule.
4. *Bond Pair*—pair of electrons shared between atoms.
5. *Lone Pair*—pair of electrons not involved in bonding.
6. *Double Bond*—two pairs of electrons shared between atoms.
7. *Triple Bond*—three pairs of electrons shared between atoms.
8. *Octet Rule*—in a covalent molecule, each atom has eight electrons around each atom.

E. *Intermolecular Forces*—forces that exist between molecules or ions and molecules.

F. *Metallic Bonding*—atoms sharing their outer electrons with many other atoms. Allows for ductility and malleability of metals. Examples include Cu, Mg, and Na. Generally a metal and metal bonding.

G. *Hydrogen Bonding*

1. Strong intermolecular forces between hydrogen with electronegative atoms, such as nitrogen, oxygen, and fluorine.

2. A dipole-dipole interaction, because of the large electronegativity differences between N-H, O-H, F-H
3. Hydrogen has a slight positive charge, while N, O, and F will have a slight negative charge.
4. Hydrogen bonding of molecules leads to higher boiling points. For example, ethanol (CH_3CH_2OH) has a higher boiling point than dimethyl ether (CH_3OCH_3) because ethanol has a O-H hydrogen bond.

Hydrogen Halide	Normal Boiling Pt, °C
HF*	19
HCl	−85
HBr	−67
HI	−35

*High BP attributed to hydrogen bonding

5. Examples of hydrogen bonding
   i. Water (H_2O)
   ii. Polymers, such as nylon, because of the N-H hydrogen bonding.

H. *van der Waals Forces*

1. Intermolecular forces between molecules that are NOT covalent or ion based
2. *Dipole/Dipole Moment*—molecule containing positive and negative ends
3. *Dipole-dipole forces*—one polar molecule interacting with another polar molecule due to positive and negative end interaction. The effect of a dipole-dipole force includes increased boiling point and solubility. The greater the forces between the molecules, the more energy must be added to separate them from each other. As the temperature is increased, molecules gain kinetic energy until the boiling point is reached. Polar molecules will dissolve other polar molecules, while non-polar molecules will dissolve non-polar molecules.

4. *London Dispersion Forces*—arise from induced dipoles that are present in all molecular substances.
    i. *Polar and Nonpolar Molecules*—polar molecules can induce a dipole that is temporary in non-polar molecules. For example, oxygen (O_2) can dissolve slightly in water since water can induce a dipole in oxygen.
    ii. *Interaction between Nonpolar Molecules*—momentary/temporary dipoles can be induced when electron clouds between nonpolar molecules overlap with each other.

I. Relationships to states, structure, and properties of matter

1. Properties of Liquids
    1. *Vaporization or evaporation*—liquid becomes a gas
    2. Vaporization is endothermic, taking in energy to separate molecules that are close to each other. The molar enthalpy of vaporization, $\Delta H°_{vap}$.
    3. High vapor pressure = volatile = weak intermolecular forces
    4. *Condensation*—when a gas reenters the liquid phase. Opposite of vaporization. Therefore it is exothermic (transfer of energy to the atmosphere).
    5. *General rules about Molar Enthalpy of Vaporization and Boiling Point*
        a. The molar enthalpy of vaporization and boiling points of non-polar liquids increase with molecular mass because of nonpolar dispersion forces.
        b.

Molecule	$\Delta H°_{vap}$ (kJ/mol)	Boiling Point °C
CH_4	8.2	−161.5
C_2H_6	14.7	−88.6
C_3H_8	19.0	−42.1
C_4H_{10}	22.4	−0.5

    6. *Vapor Pressure*—the pressure of water vapor when liquid-vapor equilibrium has been established
    7. *Volatility*—the tendency for liquid molecules to escape into the vapor phase. The higher the vapor pressure, the more volatile the substance. The higher the temperature, the higher the vapor pressure.

8. *Boiling Point*—the temperature at which vapor pressure is equal to the external pressure, if the external pressure is 1 atm.

J. Bond Polarity and Electronegativity

1. *Electronegativity*—the ability of an atom in a molecule to attract shared electrons to itself.

2. Electronegativity values can be used to predict bond type. Fluorine is the most electronegative element (4.0 value) and caesium is the least electronegative element (0.7 value).

3. General rules of electronegativity

   i. Electronegativity differences of 1.7 or more indicate an ionic bond. For example, Li (1.0) and O (3.4), the difference is 2.4.

   ii. Electronegativity differences between 1.7 and 0.4 indicate the bond is considered polar covalent. For example, N (3.0) and F (4.0), the difference is 1.0.

   iii. When electronegativity differences are below 0.4, the bond is considered to be a nonpolar covalent. For example, H (2.2) and H (2.2), the difference is 0.

4. *Dipole/Dipole Moment*—molecule containing positive and negative ends. An arrow pointing to the negative charge is the usual indication for a dipole moment.

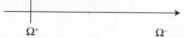

Ω^+ Ω^-

Water has a dipole moment illustrated in the following way.

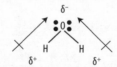

Some molecules have polar bonds, but no dipole moment because they cancel out. The best examples of such are CO_2, CCl_4, and SO_3. This is predicted by molecular geometries, including linear, planar, and tetrahedral.

K. Bond Properties

1. *Bond Length*—the average distance between the nuclei of two bonded atoms in a molecule.

2. Bond length is proportional to atom size. For example, all hydrogen halides have a bond length of the following: H – F < H – Cl < H – Br < H – I, since down a group atomic radii increase. Similarity of bond length across a period would be greater: C – N > C – O > C – F.
3. Multiple bonds with the same elements tend to decrease bond length. For example, C – C > C = C > C ≡ C.

L. Bond Energy

1. Bond Energy—measurement of the strength of a bond (an average).
2. The change in enthalpy for a reaction can be calculated using bond energies.

$$\Delta H^{o}_{rxn} = \sum \text{Bond Energy}_{\text{Reactants}} - \sum \text{Bond Energy}_{\text{Products}}$$

Sample AP Question

Based on the reaction below, determine enthalpy change using bond energies.

$$2H_2(g) + O_2(g) \rightarrow 2H_2O(g)$$

Bond	Average Bond Energy (kJ/mol)
H-H	436
O-O	499
H-O	463

$$\Delta H^{o}_{rxn} = \sum \text{Bond Energy}_{\text{Reactants}} - \sum \text{Bond Energy}_{\text{Products}}$$

$$\Delta H^{o}_{rxn} = \sum 2\left(436\frac{kJ}{mol}\right) + \left(\frac{499\ kJ}{mol}\right) - \sum 4\left(463\frac{kJ}{mol}\right)$$

$$\Delta H^{o}_{rxn} = -\frac{481\ kJ}{mol}$$

Test Tip

A substantial number of questions on the AP exam relate to bond polarity and properties. Look for clues such as periodic relationships, metal/metal bonding, or metal/non-metal bonding.

Molecular Models

I. Molecular Models

A. Rules for Drawing Lewis Structures

1. Determine the central atom.
   i. Usually the atom with lowest electronegativity
   ii. Some common central atoms: C, N, P, S
   iii. *Sometimes* the first atom, but not always
2. Determine the terminal atoms.
   i. H is always terminal since it can only bond with two electrons.
3. Determine the total valence electrons in molecule or ion.
   i. For anions, add electrons equal to the negative charge.
   ii. For cations, subtract electrons equal to the positive charge.
   iii. Example: CH_3OH

   Valence Electrons = 4 valence electrons for 1 C atom
   6 valence electrons for 1 O atom
   4 valence electrons for 4 H atoms
4. Form single bonds between atoms.
5. Any remaining electrons are placed around each terminal atom to form an octet.
   i. *Octet Rule*—atoms combine to have eight electrons in their valence shells
6. Form double or triple bonds if the central atom has less than an octet of electrons.
7. For ions, place the structure in a bracket and label with the correct charge.

B. Resonance

1. Resonance structures are used to represent the bonding of molecule or ions when more than one Lewis Structure can be drawn.
2. The actual molecule is a composite of all the resonance structures that can be drawn. This is called a *resonance hybrid*.
3. Moving atoms around and attaching them to different atoms does not create a resonance structure.

Resonance Structures of the Carbonate Ion $CO_3{}^{2-}$

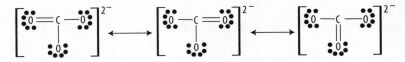

C. Sample AP Questions on Drawing Lewis Structures

1. Draw the following Lewis Structures
   i. CO_2

   O══C══O

   ii. N_2

   :N≡N:

   iii. NH_3

   H—N—H
      |
      H

   iv. $PO_4{}^{3-}$

v. NF$_3$

vi. NH$_2$OH

H—N—O—H
    |
    H

vii. CH$_3$COOH

```
        H      O
        |      ||
    H — C  —  C — O — H
        |
        H
```

viii. CH$_3$OH

```
        H
        |
    H — C — O — H
        |
        H
```

D. Exceptions to the Octet Rule

1. Molecules with fewer than 4 electron pairs

   i. Boron has three valence electrons resulting in a valence of 6 electrons rather than an octet. Examples include: BF$_3$, BCl$_3$, BBr$_3$, and BI$_3$.

```
    Cl — B — Cl
         |
         Cl
```

2. Molecules with more than 4 electron pairs
   i. Elements in the third or higher periods form expanded octets. Examples include: PF_5, SF_4, XeF_2, SF_6, BrF_5.

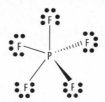

3. Molecules with odd number of electrons
   i. An odd number of electrons will result in at least one unpaired electron. Free radicals = chemical species with an unpaired electron. Examples include NO and NO_2.

There is a strong possibility that you may be required to draw a Lewis structure on free-response questions. Be neat, show bonding and free electrons, and do not forget about resonance structures.

Geometry of Molecules

I. Geometry of Molecules

A. VSEPR (Valence Shell Electron Pair Repulsion) Model

1. VSEPR is a method used to predict the shapes of covalent molecules and polyatomic ions.
2. VSEPR is based on valence shell electrons repelling each other so they are as far apart as possible.

**Molecular Geometry with
Central Atom Having No Lone Electron Pair**

Molecular Geometry	Number of lone electron pairs around central atom	Formula	Example	VSEPR Prediction and Bond Angle Measurement
Linear	0	AX_2	CO_2	180° X—A—X
Trigonal Planar	0	AX_3	BF_3	120°

Continued →

(Continued from previous page)

Molecular Geometry	Number of lone electron pairs around central atom	Formula	Example	VSEPR Prediction and Bond Angle Measurement
Tetrahedral	0	AX_4	CH_4	
Trigonal-bipyramidal	0	AX_5	PF_5	
Octahedral	0	AX_6	SF_6	

Molecular Geometry with
Central Atom Having One Lone Electron Pair

Molecular Geometry	Number of lone electron pairs around central atom	Formula	Example	VSEPR Prediction
Bent	1	AX_2E	SeO_2	
Trigonal Pyramidal	1	AX_3E	NH_3	
Seesaw	1	AX_4E	SF_4	
Square-Pyramidal	1	AX_5E	BrF_5	

Molecular Geometry with
Central Atom Having Two Lone Electron Pairs

Molecular Geometry	Number of lone electron pairs around central atom	Formula	Example	VSEPR Prediction
Bent	2	AX_2E_2	H_2O	
T-shape	2	AX_3E_2	ICl_3	
Square Planar	2	AX_4E_2	XeF_4	

Molecular Geometry with
Central Atom Having Three Lone Electron Pairs

Molecular Geometry	Number of lone electron pairs around central atom	Formula	Example	VSEPR Prediction
Linear	3	AX_2E_3	XeF_2	

B. Valence Bond Theory (VBT)

1. VBT is based on the Orbital Overlap Model or the concept that bonds are formed by the overlap of orbitals.
   i. Orbitals overlap to form bonds between atoms.
   ii. One electron from each of the bonded atoms accommodates the overlapping orbital.
   iii. Both electrons in the overlap are attracted to the nucleus of each atom. This is why electron pairs are located between two atoms in Lewis structures.

2. Sigma (σ) Bond (All Single Bonds)
   i. The overlap of two s orbitals such as in H-H bond—also called σ_s
   ii. The overlap of an s and p orbital such as in H-Cl—also called σ_{sp}
   iii. The overlap of two p orbitals such as in Cl-Cl—also called σ_p

3. Pi (π) Bond (Only in Double Bonds)
   i. The overlap of two p orbitals such as in C=C
   ii. Double bonds have 1 sigma and 1 pi bond
   iii. Triple bonds contain 1 sigma and 2 pi bonds

4. Hybrid Orbitals
   i. Formed by the blending of $s, p, d,$ and f orbitals.
   ii. Hybridization can be matched to molecular geometry/number of electrons around the central atom.

Geometry	Number of effective electrons pairs around central atom (count electron pairs double and triple bonds once)	Hybridization
Linear	2	sp
Trigonal Planar	3	sp^2
Tetrahedral	4	sp^3
Trigonal bipyramidal	5	sp^3d
Octahedral	6	sp^3d^2

Sample AP Question

Based on the molecule below, indicate the hybridization and number of sigma and pi bonds around the C and N atoms below.

$$H - \underset{\underset{H}{|}}{\overset{\overset{H}{|}}{C}} - \underset{\underset{H}{|}}{C} = N$$

with O—H group above the second carbon.

From left to right, first carbon sp³ (4σ bonds), second carbon sp² (3σ-bonds and 1 π bond), nitrogen is sp² (2σ-bonds and 1 π bond)

The key to molecular geometry is for you to MEMORIZE, MEMORIZE, MEMORIZE! Knowing all the shapes will help you earn points on the multiple-choice section of the exam.

Nuclear Chemistry

I. Nuclear Chemistry

A. Nuclear emission or transmutations—the natural change of one isotope of one element into the isotope of another element via the changing of the nucleus.

1. Unstable element is changed into a more stable one.
2. Changes the atomic number and mass number of the initial element.
3. Spontaneous decay is a hallmark of radioactive species.

B. Three types of nuclear emissions

Type	Symbol	Charge
Alpha Particle	$^{4}_{2}He$	2+
Beta Particle	$^{0}_{-1}e$, $^{0}_{-1}\beta$	1−
Gamma Particle	$^{0}_{0}\gamma$	0

C. Alpha radiation/emission

1. Protons and neutrons (nucleons) stay the same.
2. New atom is formed.
3. Sum of mass numbers and atomic numbers *must* stay the same.
4. Atomic number decreases by 2 units, and mass number decreases by 4 units.

5. Alpha particle is part of the react products.

$$^{226}_{88}Ra \rightarrow ^{4}_{2}He + ^{222}_{86}Rn$$

Mass Number $226 \rightarrow 4 + 222$
Atomic Number $88 \rightarrow 2 + 86$

6. Alpha particles have limited penetrating capability and can be stopped by ordinary means.

D. Beta radiation/emission

1. A neutron is converted into a proton.
2. Sum of mass numbers and atomic numbers *must* stay the same.
3. The atomic number of the products *must* be one greater than the reactant to balance the charge. Mass number does not change.
4. Beta particle or electron is part of the products.
5. Beta particles have higher penetrating capability than alpha particles and can easily penetrate the tissue and cells.

$$^{239}_{92}U \rightarrow ^{0}_{-1}\beta + ^{239}_{93}Np$$

Mass Number $239 \rightarrow 0 + 239$
Atomic Number $92 \rightarrow -1 + 93$

E. Gamma radiation/emission

1. A ray with no mass is given off.
2. No transmutation of the original element because the gamma ray has no appreciable mass.
3. Most penetrating of all types of emissions and requires lead or concrete for protection.

F. Radioactive decay series

1. A set/sequence of nuclear reactions that produce radioactive isotopes that will further decay.
2. Occur in uranium ores with the most common decay series being the decay of 238-Uranium.

G. Positron radiation/emission

1. Positron has equal mass to an electron and a +1 charge.
2. Leads to a decrease in atomic number.

$$^{207}_{84}\text{Po} \rightarrow ^{0}_{+1}\beta + ^{207}_{83}\text{Bi}$$

Mass Number   207 → 0 + 207
Atomic Number   84 → +1 + 83

H. Electron capture

1. Electron is captured by the nucleus
2. Leads to a decrease in atomic number.

$$^{7}_{4}\text{Be} + ^{0}_{-1}\text{e} \rightarrow ^{7}_{3}\text{Li}$$

Mass Number   7 + 0 → 7
Atomic Number   4 + −1 → 3

I. Nuclear fission

1. The nucleus of an atom splits into two or more smaller atoms.

J. Nuclear fusion

1. Lightweight atoms fuse together to form a larger atom.

Test Tip

Although this topic is light on the AP test, you can expect one or two questions on types of radioactive decays.

PART III:
STATES OF MATTER

Gases: Ideal Gases

I. Gases

A. Properties of Gases

1. Compressible
2. No definite shape or volume
3. Fill their containers
4. Occupy more space than solids or liquids
5. Exert a pressure that is measurable
6. Low densities
7. STP—Standard Temperature and Pressure
   i. Standard Temperature—0°C (273K)
   ii. Standard Pressure—1 atm = 760 mm Hg = 101.3 kPa=1.013 bar
   iii. Under STP 1 mole of *any* gas occupies 22.4 L.

B. Properties of Ideal Gases

1. Ideal Gases are "approximations" used to model the behavior of gases.
2. Based on small gas molecules (point masses) that have virtually no volume.
3. Collisions between gas molecules are "elastic." This means that kinetic energy between the gas molecules stays the same.
4. Based on gases at high temperatures and low pressure.
5. No attraction between gas molecules

6. Governed by the following parameters:
   i.   Pressure (P)
   ii. Volume (V)
   iii. Moles (n)
   iv. Temperature (T) in Kelvin (K = 273 + °C)

C. Properties of Real Gases

1. Based on gas molecules that have mass and volume.
2. Based on gases at low temperatures and high pressure.

D. Gas Pressure—the force per unit area exerted by a gas

1. $Pressure = \dfrac{Force}{Area}$
2. Common units of pressure
   i.   Millimeters of Mercury (Hg)—mmHg
   ii. Standard Atmosphere—atm
   iii. Pascal—(Pa)
   iv. Bar (bar)
   v.   1 atm = 760 mmHg = 101.3 kPa =1.013 bar
3. Reading Pressure Using a Manometer
   i.   Manometer—instrument used to measure pressure.

E. Avogadro's Law—The volume of a gas is directly proportional to the number of moles (n) of the gas, under constant temperature and pressure.

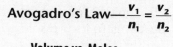

Avogadro's Law— $\dfrac{v_1}{n_1} = \dfrac{v_2}{n_2}$

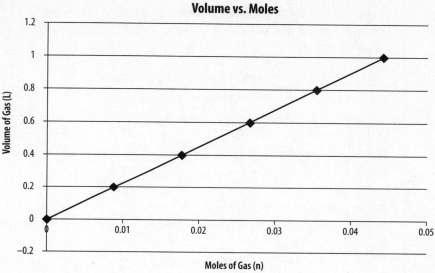

Volume vs. Moles

Sample AP Problem

An 11.1-L sample of 0.25 mol oxygen gas is converted to ozone. If all the oxygen is converted to ozone, what will the volume of ozone be?

$$3O_2 \ (g) \rightarrow 2O_3(g)$$

$$\frac{0.25 \text{ mol } O_2}{1} \times \frac{2 \text{ mol } O_3}{3 \text{ mol } O_2} = 0.17 \text{ mol } O_3$$

$$\frac{11.1 \text{ L}}{0.25 \text{ mol}} = \frac{x}{0.17 \text{ mol}}$$

$$x = 7.5 \text{ L}$$

F. Boyle's Law—The volume of a gas at a fixed temperature is inversely proportional to its pressure.

1. Pressure—volume product of one condition is equal to that of another set of conditions under constant temperature and quantity of gas.

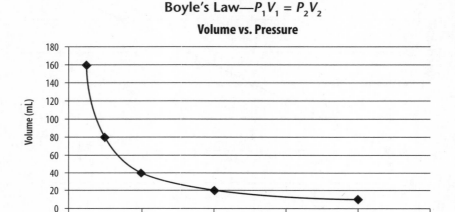

Boyle's Law—$P_1V_1 = P_2V_2$

Volume vs. Pressure

> Note in the graph above that when the pressure is doubled, the volume is halved. Therefore, the mathematics of solving a Boyle's Law problem is easy.

Sample AP Question

If the pressure of a gas with a volume of 300 mL is tripled, what is the new volume?

Answer: 1/3 of 300 mL or 100 mL.

Many students think the question is not answerable because no pressure is given. Know your concepts!!!!

G. Charles's Law—The volume of a gas at a fixed pressure is directly proportional to its temperature in degrees Kelvin.

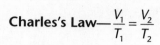

$$\text{Charles's Law—}\frac{V_1}{T_1} = \frac{V_2}{T_2}$$

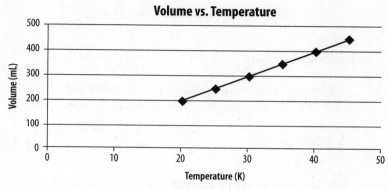

Note in the graph above that when the temperature is doubled, the volume is doubled. Therefore, the mathematics of solving a Charles's Law problem is easy.

Sample AP Question

If the temperature of a gas with a volume of 200 mL is doubled, what is the new volume?

Answer: Double 200 mL to 400 mL

Many students think the question is not answerable because no pressure is given. Know your concepts!!!!

H. The Combined Gas Law (combination of Boyle's and Charles's Laws)—used when the parameters of volume, temperature, and pressure change. The amount, or number of moles, of the gas stays the same.

$$\text{Combined Gas Law—} \frac{V_1 P_1}{T_1} = \frac{V_2 P_2}{T_2}$$

Sample AP Problem

A 200 cm³ sample of helium gas is collected at 25.0°C and 97.4 kPa. What volume would this gas occupy at STP?

$V_1 = 200 \text{ cm}^3$

$P_1 = 97.4 \text{ kPa}$

$T_1 = $ (must convert to Kelvin)
    $25 + 273 = 298\text{K}$

$V_2 = ?$

$P_2 = 101.1 \text{ kPa}$

$T_2 = 273\text{K}$

$V_2 = 177 \text{ cm}^3$

$$\frac{(200 \text{ cm}^3)(97.4 \text{ kPa})}{(298\text{K})} = \frac{(V_2)(101.1\text{kPa})}{(273\text{K})}$$

I. The Ideal Gas Law—

1. Formula for the Ideal Gas Law = PV=nRT (R=gas law constant).

   i. R or the gas law constant is derived by solving for R under STP conditions

   $$R = \frac{PV}{nT} = \left(\frac{(1 \text{ atm})(22.4 \text{ L})}{(1 \text{ mol})(273.15 \text{ K})} \right) = 0.0821 \frac{L \cdot atm}{K \cdot mol}$$

   ii. An equation that is used for the gas in its given conditions, and not changing conditions.

   iii. Need three of the four variables to be able to use the equation.

Type 1 Ideal Gas Law (basic and straightforward)	A sample of oxygen gas has a volume of 4.5 L at standard temperature and 1.3 atm? Calculate the number of moles of oxygen. $$(1.3 \ atm)(4.5 \ L) = (n)\left(0.0821\frac{L \cdot atm}{K \cdot mol}\right)(273K)$$ $$n = 0.26 \ mol$$
Type 2 Ideal Gas Law (conversion to moles)	If a 3.0-L container is filled with 474 g of Ne gas at 5 atm, what is the temperature? 474 g Ne = 23.5 *mol* Ne $$(5.0 \ atm)(3.0 \ L) = (23.5 \ mol)\left(0.0821\frac{L \cdot atm}{K \cdot mol}\right)(T)$$ $$T = 7.8 \ K$$
Type 3 Ideal Gas Law (calculating the molar mass)	A sample of 0.413g of an ideal gas at 200 K and 1.20 atm has a volume of 1.50-L. What is the molar mass of the gas? $$(1.20 \ atm)(1.50 \ L) = (n)\left(0.0821\frac{L \cdot atm}{K \cdot mol}\right)(200 \ K)$$ $$n = 0.11 \ mol$$ $$Molar \ Mass = \frac{0.413 \ g}{0.11 \ mol} = 3.8\frac{g}{mol}$$
Type 4 Ideal Gas Law (combining volumes)	A 5.00-L sealed jar at 20 °C contains 0.120 moles of oxygen and 0.120 moles of hydrogen gas. What is the pressure in the container? $$(P)(5.00 \ L) = (0.240 \ mol)\left(0.0821\frac{L \cdot atm}{K \cdot mol}\right)(293 \ K)$$ $$P = 1.15 \ atm$$

H. Density of Gases

1. Density is defined as mass per unit volume: $Density = \dfrac{mass}{volume}$.

2. Density, Molar Mass (MM), and the Ideal Gas Law can be combined in the following way: $Density = \dfrac{mass}{volume} = \dfrac{PMM}{RT}$

Sample AP Problem

The density of an unknown gas at STP is 0.870 g/L. Find the molar mass of the gas.

$$0.870 \frac{g}{L} = \frac{(1\,atm)(MM)}{\left(0.0821\dfrac{L \cdot atm}{K \cdot mol}\right)(273\,K)}$$

$$MM = 19.5\frac{g}{mol}$$

Sample AP Problem

At 1.0 atmosphere and 0°C, calculate the density of NO_2 gas ($MM = 46.0$ g/mol).

Key is STP (1 mole of any gas at STP = 22.4 L)

$$\frac{46.0\,g\,/\,mol}{22.4\,L\,/\,mol} = 2.05\frac{g}{L}$$

J. Molar Mass Calculation from Gas Data

   1. Use PV = nRT and the definition of molar mass.

Sample AP Problem

0.20 g of a 1.00-L gas exerts a pressure of 1.2 *atm* at 27.4°C. Find the molar mass of the compound.

$$(1.20\ atm)(1.00\ L) = (n)\left(0.0821\frac{L \cdot atm}{K \cdot mol}\right)(300.4\ K)$$

$$n = 0.049\ mol$$

$$\frac{0.20\,g}{0.049\,mol} = 4.1\frac{g}{mol}$$

K. Gas Stoichiometry

1. Flow chart

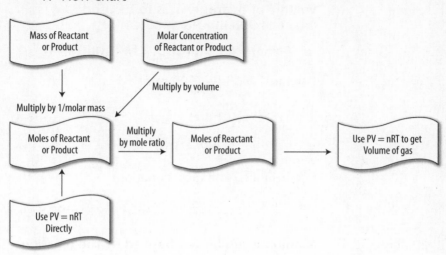

Type 1	**An excess of Mg(s) is added to 100 mL of 0.300 *M* HF. At 0°C and 1 *atm* pressure, what is the volume of hydrogen gas produced?** Write the balanced chemical equation first
	$$Mg\ (s) + 2\ HF\ (aq) \rightarrow MgF_2(aq) + H_2\ (g)$$
	Use stoichiometry
	$$\frac{0.1\,L\,HF}{1} \times \frac{0.300\,mol\,HF}{1\,L\,HF} \times \frac{1\,mol\,H_2}{2\,mol\,HF} = 0.015\,mol\,H_2$$
	1 mol of any gas at STP=22.4 L
	$$\frac{0.015\,mol\,H_2}{1} \times \frac{22.4\,L\,H_2}{1\,mol\,H_2} = 0.34\,L\,H_2$$

Continued →

(Continued from previous page)

Type 2	**What quantity of Fe should be used if the volume of hydrogen gas to be produced is 21.3 L at 900 mmHg at 30°C?**
	2 Fe(s) + 6 HCl(aq) → 2 FeCl$_3$(aq) +3 H$_2$(g)
	Use Ideal Gas Law (900 mmHg = 1.18 *atm*)
	$(1.18\ atm)(21.3\ L) = (n)\left(0.0821\dfrac{L\cdot atm}{K\cdot mol}\right)(303\ K)$
	$n = 1.01\ mol\ H_2$
	Use balanced chemical equations
	$\dfrac{1.01\,mol\,H_2}{1}\times\dfrac{2\,mol\,Fe}{3\,mol\,H_2} = 0.673\,mol\,Fe\ or\ 37.6\ g\ Fe$
Type 3	**Ammonia can be synthesized by the reaction below:**
	N$_2$(g)+3H$_2$(g) → 2NH$_3$(g)
	If you have 450 L of nitrogen gas at 25°C and 800 mmHg and combine it with excess hydrogen, how many moles of ammonia are produced?
	Use Ideal Gas Law (800 mmHg=1.05 atm)
	$(1.05\ atm)(450\ L) = (n)\left(0.0821\dfrac{L\cdot atm}{K\cdot mol}\right)(298\ K)$
	$n = 19.3\ mol\ N_2$
	Use balanced chemical equations
	$\dfrac{19.3\,mol\,N_2}{1}\times\dfrac{2\,mol\,NH_3}{1\,mol\,N_2} = 38.6\,mol\,NH_3$
	If the ammonia is stored in a 100. L container at 25°C, what is the pressure exerted by the gas?
	Use Ideal Gas Law
	$(P)(100\ L) = (38.6\ mol\ NH_3)\left(0.0821\dfrac{L\cdot atm}{K\cdot mol}\right)(298\ K)$
	$P = 9.44\ atm$

L. Dalton's Law of Partial Pressure

1. The pressure of each gas in a mixture of gases exerts a pressure that is equal to the fractional part of the whole.

   i. $P_{Total} = P_A + P_B + P_C + \ldots\ldots$

2. Each gas behaves independently from one another in the mixture and the pressure exerted by each gas can be calculated.

   i. $P_A V = n_A RT$—pressure exerted by gas A

   ii. $P_B V = n_B RT$—pressure exerted by gas B

   iii. $P_C V = n_C RT$—pressure exerted by gas C

3. The total pressure in the mixture is calculated using the sum of the pressures.

   i. $P_{Total} V = n_{Total} RT$

4. Mole Fraction (X)—the number of moles of a particular substance divided by the total number of moles.

   i. $X_a = \dfrac{n_a}{n_a + n_b + n_c} = \dfrac{n_a}{n_{total}}$

   ii. If you know the total pressure of the mixture of gases you can multiply it by the mole fraction to calculate the partial pressure of the gas: $P_A = X_a P_{total}$

Sample AP Problem

A mixture of 43.2 g of oxygen gas and 22.1 g of carbon dioxide are contained in a vessel exerting a total pressure of 980 mmHg. Find the pressure exerted by each gas.

$$43.2 \ g \ O_2 = 1.35 \ mol \ O_2$$

$$22.1 \ g \ CO_2 = 0.502 \ mol \ CO_2$$

$$\text{Total moles} = 1.85 \ mol$$

$$P_{O_2} = \frac{1.35 \ mol \ O_2}{1.85 \ mol}(980 \ mm \ Hg) = 715 \ mmHg$$

$$P_{CO_2} = 980 \ mmHg - 715 \ mmHg = 265 \ mmHg$$

5. Collecting a Gas Over Water
    i. In the apparatus below, the gas collecting chamber (test tube) contains both water vapor and the gas of interest. Evolved gas from the chemical reaction in the flask displaces water. As water is pushed out and the gas is collected, a water vapor pressure is exerted.

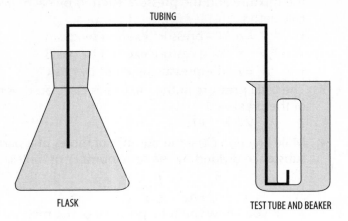

TUBING

FLASK

TEST TUBE AND BEAKER

Sample AP Problem

41.5 L of N_2 gas is collected over water at 23.0°C. The total pressure of the gases in the collecting flask is 775 mmHg. What is the mass of N_2 collected? (At 23.0°C, the vapor pressure of water=0.028 atm)

(Dalton's Law of Partial Pressure)

$$775 \text{ mmHg} = 1.02 \text{ atm} = P_{N_2} + P_{H_2O}$$

Use Ideal Gas Law to Find Total Moles

$$(1.02 \text{ atm})(41.5 \text{ L}) = (n)\left(0.0821\frac{L \cdot atm}{K \cdot mol}\right)(296 \text{ K})$$

$$n = 1.74 \text{ mol (total)}$$

At 23.0°C vapor pressure of water = 0.028 atm

$$1.02 \text{ atm} = P_{N_2} + 0.028 \text{ atm}$$

$$P_{N_2} = 0.99 \text{ atm}$$

Use Ideal Gas Law to Find Mass of N_2 collected

$$(0.99 \; atm)(41.5 \; L) = (n)\left(0.0821\frac{L \cdot atm}{K \cdot mol}\right)(296 \; K)$$
$$n = 1.69 \; mol \; N_2 = 47 \; g \; N_2$$

Alternate Solution By Using Mole Fraction

$$\frac{.99 \; atm \; N_2}{1.02 \; total \; atm} \times 1.74 \; mol \; total = 1.69 \; mol \; N_2 = 47 \; g \; N_2$$

Test Tip

Gases are one of the major topics on the AP Chemistry exam. The Ideal Gas Law and Gas Stoichiometry have a high probability of being on the exam. Be sure you can write a balanced chemical equation and use it in relation to the laws.

Gases: Kinetic Molecular Theory

I. Gases: Kinetic Molecular Theory

A. The Kinetic Molecular Theory of Gases

1. Kinetic Energy (KE) is defined as the energy of motion.

$$KE = \frac{1}{2} mass \cdot velocity^2$$

2. The KE of a gas is directly proportional to the temperature. The higher the temperature, the faster the speed of the gas molecules (the greater the KE).

3. Gases consist of molecules whose distance between each other is greater than the size of the gas molecule.

4. Gas molecules are in continuous, random, and rapid motion.

5. Gas molecules collide with each other and the walls of the vessel that contains them. During the collision no energy is lost, therefore they are elastic collisions.

6. Gases with different molecular masses *must* have the same average kinetic energy at the same temperature. Heavier gases must travel more slowly, while lighter gases travel faster.

B. Speeds of Gases

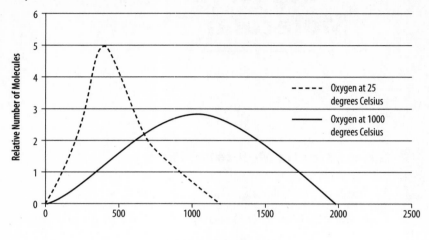

1. The data above indicates the following relating to the speed of gases

   i.   At a given temperature, gas molecules have high and low speeds, but all achieve a common speed or maximum speed (peak of curve).

   ii. As temperature increases, the common speed increases.

   iii. As the temperature increases, many more molecules are traveling faster. For example, at 1000°C, molecules can be traveling between 1500 and 2000 m/s, while at 25°C they cannot.

   iv. Mean Square Speed or rms speed ($\sqrt{u^2}$), temperature (T, in Kelvin), and molar mass (*MM*) are related (Maxwell's Equation).

$$\sqrt{u^2} = \sqrt{\frac{3RT}{MM}}$$

2. Diffusion
   i. The mixing of gas molecules as a result of random motion.
   ii. Given time, gaseous components of one mixture will interact with the gaseous components of another mixture.
3. Effusion
   i. The movement of gas molecules through tiny openings from one container into another container.
   ii. Graham's Law of Effusion

$$\frac{\text{Rate of effusion of gas 1}}{\text{Rate of effusion of gas 2}} = \sqrt{\frac{\text{molar mass of gas 2}}{\text{molar mass of gas 1}}}$$

Sample Calculation

$$\frac{\text{Rate of effusion of } H_2}{\text{Rate of effusion of gas } O_2} = \sqrt{\frac{32.00}{2.02}} = \frac{3.98}{1}$$

Hydrogen will effuse 3.98 times faster than oxygen.

C. Avogadro's Hypothesis and the Mole Concept

1. Equal volumes of gases at the same temperature and pressure contain the same number of molecules regardless of their chemical nature and physical properties.

   The number of molecules is 6.022×10^{23} or 22.4 L in volume at standard temperature and pressure.

Sample AP Problem

Three containers are all filled with equal volumes of three separate gases, O_2, CO_2, and N_2. All the containers are at the same temperature and pressure.

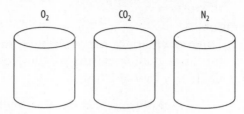

O_2 CO_2 N_2

(A) Which container has the least mass? All contain the same number of molecules, but since N_2 has the smallest molar mass it has the least mass.

(B) Which container has the greatest velocity? Since N_2 is the lightest, it is traveling the fastest.

(C) Which container has the greatest kinetic energy? All have the same kinetic energy because they are at the same temperature.

(D) Which gas would leak the fastest out of a hole in the container? N_2 would leak the fastest since it has the smallest molar mass. Graham's Law is used to make this prediction.

Test Tip

Not all gas questions require calculations. Being able to use the concept of the Kinetic Molecular Theory to describe the behavior of gases will be helpful for the AP Chemistry free-response questions.

Liquids and Solids

I. Liquids and Solids

A. Kinetic Molecular Viewpoint

1. Liquids

   i. Very little order in structure. Have a definite volume, but take the shape of their container.

   ii. *Vaporization* is the process by which molecules move from a liquid to a gas state. The higher the temperature, the higher the kinetic energy of a liquid to escape into the gas phase.

   iii. Vaporization is highly endothermic, since energy must be adsorbed by the liquid molecules to break free from one another.

   iv. *Molar enthalpy of vaporization, $\Delta H°_{vap}$,* is defined as the amount of energy required to vaporize a sample of liquid.

   v. *Condensation* is defined as the process in which gases re-enter the liquid state. Condensation is the opposite of vaporization and, therefore, is exothermic, releasing energy. The enthalpy change is equal in magnitude but opposite in sign to the molar enthalpy of vaporization.

   vi. *Critical point* is the point at which a specific temperature and pressure are reached and a boundary between the liquid and gas state no longer exist. The vapor pressure curve ceases to exist further past this point. This is accomplished at very high temperatures and pressures. Critical pressure (P_c) and critical temperature (T_c) are the points in which this exists. Critical temperature is the lowest temperature above which a substance cannot be liquefied at any applied pressure.

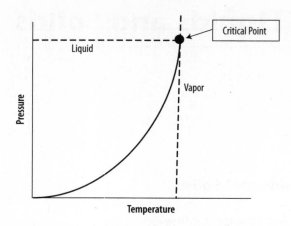

vii. *Surface tension*—The energy required to break the surface of a liquid.

viii. *Viscosity*—Measurement of the resistance of a liquid to flow. Water has a low viscosity, while honey has a high viscosity.

ix. *Adhesion*—Attractive forces that exist between different molecules.

x. *Cohesion*—Attraction between like molecules (intermolecular).

2. Solids

i. Have definite shape and volume.

ii. Molecules that make up solids, do move, but at a very slow rate.

iii. *Unit cell*—The smallest unit of a crystalline solid.

iv. *Lattice point*—corner of a unit cell

Type of Solids	Example	Structure
Ionic	NaCl	Cation/anion interaction
Metallic	Gold	Metal cations
Molecular	CH_4	Covalent Bonding
Amorphous	Glass	Atoms held together
Network	Diamond	Covalent network

v. *Melting point*—The temperature at which the solid is converted to a liquid.

vi. *Molar enthalpy of fusion*, $\Delta H^{\circ}_{fusion}$, is defined as the amount of energy needed for melting.

vii. *Molar enthalpy of crystallization*—The energy required to freeze a liquid to a solid. The enthalpy change is equal in magnitude, but opposite in sign, to the molar enthalpy of fusion.

viii. *Sublimation*—defines molecules that go directly from the solid to gas state.

3. Phase diagrams and one-component systems

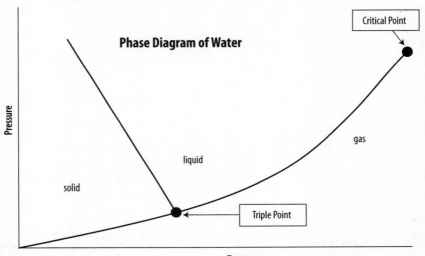

i. *Phase Diagram*—illustration depicting the conditions in which the state of matter of a molecule can exist depending on pressure and temperature.

ii. Any point on the solid/liquid line indicates the melting point of the substance at a given temperature and pressure.

iii. Any point on the liquid/gas line indicates the boiling point of the substance at a given temperature and pressure.

iv. *Triple Point*—point at which all three phases exist.

v. All normal boiling points and melting points would be based on 1 atmosphere of pressure.

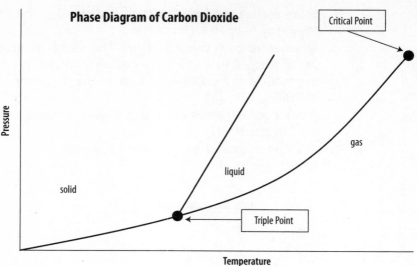

Phase Diagram of Carbon Dioxide

Critical Point

Pressure

gas

liquid

solid

Triple Point

Temperature

NOTE THE PHASE DIAGRAM FOR CARBON DIOXIDE HAS
A POSITIVE SLOPE FOR ITS LIQUID-SOLID LINE. MOST
SUBSTANCES, OTHER THAN WATER, BEHAVE IN THIS MANNER.

Test Tip

*Understanding a phase diagram is a must for the AP Chemistry
test. Do not be surprised if you need to use graphical analysis
to find areas of melting, freezing, condensation, or boiling.
This is a classic AP Chemistry multiple-choice question.*

Solutions

I. Solutions

A. Types of solutions and factors affecting solubility

1. *Saturated solution*—a solution in which the maximum amount of solute has been dissolved. Additional solute that is added to the solution will not dissolve and will remain at the bottom of the container.

2. *Supersaturated solution*—a solution that contains more of the dissolved material than could be dissolved by the solvent under normal circumstances. Conditions that allow for a supersaturated solution include changes in temperature, volume, or pressure.

3. *Unsaturated solution*—a solution that contains less than the maximum amount of solute that can be dissolved.

4. If two liquids mix to form a solution they are called *miscible*. If they cannot mix to any appreciable amount, they are called *immiscible*.

   i. Polar compounds will dissolve in polar compounds: "Like dissolves like."

   ii. Non-polar compounds will dissolve in non-polar compounds: "Like dissolves like."

   iii. Polar compounds are immiscible with non-polar compounds.

5. The "like dissolves like" property can be expanded to solids dissolving in liquids.

6. The solubility of a gas in a liquid is directly proportional to the pressure of the gas. An example of such includes carbonated soda, which contains carbon dioxide gas that is dissolved under intense pressure.

7. The solubility of all gases in water decreases with increasing temperature. An example of such is when carbonated drinks go "flat" with increased temperature. Dissolved gas molecules escape at higher temperatures because of increased kinetic energy. Similarly, at lower temperatures, the same molecules are not moving as fast and therefore stay dissolved in the solution.

8. Heating a solute in a solution increases solubility. Heat moves the molecules apart from each other, expediting the solvation process.

9. Mixing a solute within a solution increases solubility. Movement separates the molecules from each other and expedites the solvation process.

B. Solubility Curves

1. A graphical analysis is used to determine the mass of a solute in 100g (100 mL) of water at a given temperature.

2. A saturated solution is represented as any point on the line.

3. An unsaturated solution is represented as any point below the line.

4. A supersaturated solution is represented as any point above the line, and when cooled, the amount of precipitate can be determined.

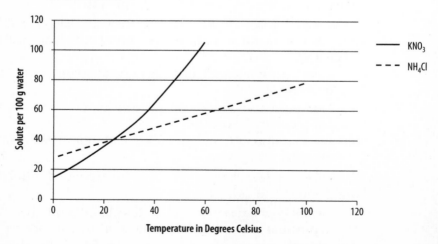

C. Methods for expressions of concentration units

1. $Molarity\ (M) = \dfrac{moles\ of\ solute}{liters\ of\ solution}$

   Sample AP Problem—Determine the mass of KNO_3 (MM = 101 g/mol) required to prepare 100 mL of a .250 M solution

   $$\dfrac{0.10L\ KNO_3}{1} \times \dfrac{0.250\ mol\ KNO_3}{1L\ KNO_3} \times \dfrac{101\ g\ KNO_3}{1\ mol\ KNO_3} = 2.5\ g\ KNO_3$$

2. $Molarity\ (m) = \dfrac{moles\ of\ solute}{kilograms\ of\ solvent}$

   Sample AP Problem—Determine the molality of an aqueous solution of KNO_3 (MM = 101 g/mol) that has a density of 2.0 g/L.

   $$2.0\ g\ KNO_3 = 0.020\ mol\ KNO_3$$

   $$Molarity\ (m) = \dfrac{0.020\ mol\ KNO_3}{1\ kg\ of\ water} = 0.020\ m\ KNO_3$$

3. $Weight\ Percent = \dfrac{mass\ of\ substance}{total\ mass}$

   Sample AP Problem—What is the mole fraction of propanol in an aqueous solution that is 60% propanol by mass? (MM of propanol is 60 g/mol, and water is 18 g/mol.)

   $$60\%\ propanol = 60\ g\ propanol = 1\ mole\ propanol$$

   $$40\%\ water = 40\ g\ water = 2.2\ mole\ propanol$$

   $$Mole\ fraction\ of\ propanol = \dfrac{1\ mole\ propanol}{3.2\ mole\ total} = 0.31$$

D. Raoult's Law and colligative properties

1. *Colligative properties*—properties of a solution that depend on the amount of solute, *not* the type of solute particles. Includes vapor pressure, boiling point, freezing point, and osmotic pressure.

2. *Raoult's Law*—when solute is added to a solvent, vapor pressure is lowered. At the surface of the liquid there is less solvent that can escape into the atmosphere because solute molecules have displaced them at the surface. The relationship between the vapor pressure and the number of solvent molecules is a direct proportion that relates to the mole fraction of the solvent.

$$P_{solvent} = X_{solvent} \cdot P^{\circ}_{solvent}$$

$P_{solvent}$ = *vapor pressure of solvent*

$X_{solvent}$ = *mole fraction of solvent*

$P^{\circ}_{solvent}$ = *vapor pressure of pure solvent*

3. Boiling Point Elevation—the boiling point of a solution is raised relative to the amount of pure solvent. The elevation in the boiling point is directly proportionate to the molality of the solution. Since a higher temperature is needed for the vapor pressure to reach the surrounding pressure, the boiling point is elevated.

$$Elevation\ of\ boiling\ point = \Delta t_{bp} = K_{bp} \cdot m_{solute} \cdot i$$

K_{bp} = *molal boiling point constant*

m_{solute} = *molality of solute*

i = *van't Hoff factor*

4. Freezing Point Depression—the freezing point of a solution is lowered relative to the amount of pure solvent. The depression in the freezing point is directly proportional to the molality of the solution. The solute disrupts solvent-solvent solid formation, therefore the temperature must be lowered further to form a solid.

$$Depressing\ of\ freezing\ point = \Delta t_{fp} = K_{fp} \cdot m_{solute} \cdot i$$

K_{fp} = *molal freezing point constant*

m_{solute} = *molality of solute*

i = *van't Hoff factor*

5. *Osmosis*—diffusion of water through a semi-permeable membrane, from a low concentrated solution to a high concentrated solution.

6. Osmotic pressure

$$\Pi = cRT$$

$c = molar\ concentration$

$R = gas\ law\ constant$

$T = temperature\ in\ Kelvin$

Colligative properties are used to determine the molar mass of compounds, as evident in required AP Lab 4: Molar Mass by Freezing Point Depression.

PART IV:
REACTIONS

Reaction Types

I. Reaction Types

A. Acid-base reactions

1. *Arrhenius Acid*—a substance that contains hydrogen and releases hydrogen ion (H^+). Limited to aqueous solutions.
$$H_xB \rightarrow xH^+ + B^{x-}$$

2. *Arrhenius Base*—a substance that releases hydroxide (OH^-) when placed in water. Limited to aqueous solutions.
$$X(OH)_y \rightarrow X^{y+} + yOH^-$$

3. *Neutralization Reactions*
    i. Arrhenius Acid and Arrhenius Base react to produce a salt and water.
    $$HCl\ (aq) + NaOH(aq) \rightarrow H_2O\ (l) + NaCl(aq)$$
    ii. Happen between strong acids and strong bases.

4. *Brønsted-Lowry Acid*—a substance that can donate a proton, or what is called a proton donor.
$$H_3PO_4(aq) + H_2O(l) \rightarrow H_2PO_4^-(aq) + H_3O^+(aq).$$
In this reaction the acid H_3PO_4 is donating a proton (H^+) to water.
    i. A Brønsted-Lowry Acid can be a neutral compound or an ion (cation or anion).

5. *Brønsted-Lowry Base*—a substance that can accept a proton, or what is called a proton acceptor.
$$NH_3(aq) + H_2O(l) \rightarrow NH_4^+(aq) + OH^-(aq)$$
In this reaction the base NH_3 is accepting a proton (H^+) from water.
    i. A Brønsted-Lowry Base can be a neutral compound or an ion (cation or anion).

6. *Monoprotic Acids*
   i.   Can only donate one proton per molecule.
   ii. Examples include HCl, HF, CH_3COOH.
7. *Polyprotic Acids*
   i.   Can donate more than one proton per molecule.
   ii. Examples include H_2SO_4, H_3PO_4.
   iii. Anions of polyprotic acids are: SO_4^{2-}, PO_4^{3-}, CO_3^{2-} and $C_2O_4^{2-}$.
8. *Amphiprotic Substances*
   i.   Can act as either an acid or a base.
   ii. Examples include H_2O, HCO_3^-, $H_2PO_4^-$.
     ▸ Water is one of the most common examples on the AP test.
$$H_2O(l) + H_2O(l) \leftrightarrow H_3O^+(aq) + OH^-(aq)$$
9. *Conjugate Acid-Base Pairs*
   i.   A pair of compounds that differ by the presence and absence of a proton (H^+).
   ii. Conjugate acid—the partner of the Brønsted-Lowry Base.
   iii. Conjugate base—the partner of the Brønsted-Lowry Acid.
   iv. All acid-base reactions involving proton transfer have two conjugate acid-base pairs.

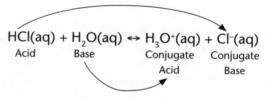

$$HCl(aq) + H_2O(aq) \leftrightarrow H_3O^+(aq) + Cl^-(aq)$$

Acid   Base   Conjugate   Conjugate
                 Acid   Base

Sample AP Questions

(1) In the following chemical reactions determine the 2 conjugate acid-base pairs.

$$C_5H_5N(aq) + CH_3COOH(aq) \leftrightarrow CH_3COO^-(aq) + C_5H_5NH^+(aq)$$

C_5H_5N (base) $C_5H_5NH^+$ (conjugate acid)

CH_3COOH (acid), CH_3COO^- (conjugate base)

(2) What is the conjugate base of H_2S?

HS⁻ (H_2S must be the acid, and lose a proton)

(3) What is the conjugate acid of CO_3^{2-}?

HCO_3^- (CO_3^{2-} must be the base, and gain an proton)

10. *Using the Brønsted-Lowry Model*
    i.   The strength of an acid and a base can be determined by the percent of ionization.
    ii. HCl is a strong Brønsted-Lowry acid since it ionizes 100% to produce H_3O^+ and Cl⁻ in water. The molar concentrations of H_3O^+ and Cl⁻ are equal to the molar concentration of HCl. For example, if the concentration of HCl is 0.25 M, then the concentrations of H_3O^+ and Cl⁻ are 0.25 M.
    iii. NH_3 is a weak base and does not ionize completely in water. Hence, the concentration of OH⁻ is much less than the initial concentration of NH_3.
    iv. The Brønsted-Lowry model predicts the stronger the acid, the weaker the conjugate base and vice versa.

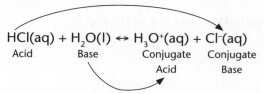

$$HCl(aq) + H_2O(l) \leftrightarrow H_3O^+(aq) + Cl^-(aq)$$
Acid   Base   Conjugate   Conjugate
                           Acid   Base

HCl is a stronger acid than H_3O^+, because it is better in donating H^+.

11. *Lewis Acid*—a substance that can accept a pair of electrons.
12. *Lewis Base*—a substance that can donate a pair of electrons.
13. *Strong Acids*—completely ionizes in water, forming hydronium or the hydrogen ion, a strong electrolyte.
14. *Strong Bases*—completely ionizes in water, forming the hydroxide ion, a strong electrolyte.
15. *Weak Acids and Weak Bases*—do not completely ionize in water; considered weak electrolytes.

Strong Acids	Strong Bases	Weak Acids	Weak Bases
HCl Hydrochloric acid	LiOH Lithium hydroxide	H_3PO_4 Phosphoric Acid	*NH_3 Ammonia
HBr Hydrobromic acid	NaOH Sodium Hydroxide	CH_3COOH Acetic Acid	
HI Hydroiodic acid	KOH Potassium Hydroxide	H_2CO_3 Carbonic Acid	
HNO_3 Nitric acid			
H_2SO_4 Sulfuric Acid			

*NH_3 as a base reacts in the following manner:

$$NH_3 + H_2O(l) \rightarrow NH_4^+(aq) + OH^-(aq)$$

II. Precipitation Reactions

A. Precipitate

1. An insoluble product
2. Reactants are generally water-soluble ionic compounds that will dissociate into anions and cations.
3. The combination of one of the anions and one of the cations will produce the precipitate.
   i. The most common example of a precipitation reaction is between silver nitrate and potassium chloride.

   $$AgNO_3(aq) + KCl(aq) \rightarrow AgCl(s) + KNO_3(aq)$$

Test Tip

Be able to write a precipitation reaction correctly. Solubility rules must be known.

B. Net Ionic Equation

1. *Spectator Ions*—ions that are found on both sides of the reaction because they are aqueous.

2. Spectator ions are *not* involved in the formation of the precipitate and the net reaction. They must be removed when writing the net ionic equation.

3. *Net Ionic Equation*—the balanced chemical equation that is written leaving out the spectator ions.

Example of Writing a Net Ionic Equation

Step 1: Balance the chemical equation

$$2AgNO_3(aq) + CaCl_2(aq) \rightarrow 2AgCl(s) + Ca(NO_3)_2(aq)$$

Step 2: Write the aqueous ions on both sides of the equation

$$2Ag^+(aq) + 2NO_3^-(aq) + Ca^{2+}(aq) + 2Cl^-(aq)$$
$$\rightarrow 2AgCl(s) + Ca^{2+}(aq) + 2NO_3^-(aq)$$

Step 3: Locate the spectator ions and remove them from the equation

$$Ag^+(aq) + Cl^-(aq) \rightarrow AgCl(s)$$

Hint: Balance the atoms as well as the charge.

AP Practice Questions

Write the net ionic equation for the following:

(1) $2KI(aq) + Pb(NO_3)_2(aq) \rightarrow 2KNO_3(aq) + PbI_2(s)$

$$2K^+(aq) + 2I^-(aq) + Pb^{2+}(aq) + 2NO_3^-(aq)$$
$$\rightarrow 2K^+(aq) + 2NO_3^-(aq) + PbI_2(s)$$

$Pb^{2+}(aq) + 2I^-(aq) \rightarrow PbI_2(s)$
(Spectator Ions K^+ and NO_3^- removed)

(2) $Ba(NO_3)_2(aq) + Na_2C_2O_4(aq)$
   $\rightarrow BaC_2O_4(s) + NaNO_3(aq)$

$Ba(NO_3)_2(aq) + Na_2C_2O_4(aq)$
   $\rightarrow BaC_2O_4(s) + 2NaNO_3(aq)$

$Ba^{2+}(aq) + 2NO_3^-(aq) + 2Na^+(aq) + C_2O_4^{2-}(aq)$
   $\rightarrow 2Na^+(aq) + 2NO_3^-(aq) + BaC_2O_4(s)$

$Ba^{2+}(aq) + C_2O_4^{2-}(aq) \rightarrow BaC_2O_4(s)$
(Spectator Ions Na^+ and NO_3^- removed)

III. Oxidation-reduction reactions

A. Oxidation Number—See Chapter 2, Part G.

B. The role of the electron in oxidation-reduction (REDOX reactions)

1. All REDOX reactions involve the transfer of electrons.
2. If a substance accepts an electron, it is *reduced.*
3. If a substance loses an electron, it is *oxidized.*
4. *Reducing Agent*—the element or compound that reduces another element or compound. In doing so, it becomes *oxidized. Reducing agent = loss in electrons.*
5. *Oxidizing Agent*—the element or compound that oxidizes another element or compound. In doing so, it becomes *reduced. Oxidizing agent = gain in electrons.*

Test Tip

Mnemonic to remember for REDOX reactions: "LEO the lion GERS" (Lost of electron oxidation . . . Gain of electron is reduction).

6. In order to determine the oxidizing and reducing agents, write the net ionic equation.

> **Ag^+ accepts electrons from Cu and is reduced to Ag**
>
> **Ag^+ is the oxidizing agent.**

$$2Ag^+(aq) + Cu(s) \rightarrow 2Ag(s) + Cu^{2+}(aq)$$

> **Cu donates electrons to Ag^+ and is oxidized to Cu^{2+}**
>
> **Cu is the reducing agent.**

Sample AP Question

Determine the oxidizing and reducing agents in the following reaction:

$$Cu(SO_4)_2(aq) + Na(s) \rightarrow Na_2SO_4(aq) + Cu(s)$$

$$Cu^{2+}(aq) + 2Na(s) \rightarrow 2Na^+(aq) + Cu(s)$$

Cu^{2+} is being reduced, therefore it is the oxidizing agent.

Na is being oxidized, therefore it is the reducing agent.

C. Balancing REDOX Reactions

1. Write the half-reactions or the reduction reaction separate from the oxidation reaction.
2. Balance atoms for each half-reaction.
3. Balance charge for each half-reaction.

> **In acidic conditions, balance oxygen with H_2O and hydrogen with H^+.**
>
> **In basic conditions, balance oxygen with OH^- and hydrogen with H_2O.**

4. Multiply each half-reaction by a coefficient, if needed.
5. Add the half-reactions.

Simple REDOX Example:
$$Cr^{2+} (aq) + I_2 (aq) \rightarrow Cr^{3+} + I^-(aq)$$

Oxidation: $Cr^{2+} (aq) \rightarrow Cr^{3+} + e^-$
Reduction: $2e^- + I_2 (aq) \rightarrow 2I^-(aq)$

Multiply Oxidation Half-Reaction by 2
$$2Cr^{2+} (aq) \rightarrow 2Cr^{3+} + 2 e^-$$
$$\underline{2e^- + I_2 (aq) \rightarrow 2I^-(aq)}$$
$$2Cr^{2+} (aq) + I_2 (aq) \rightarrow 2Cr^{3+} + 2I^-(aq)$$

Balance REDOX in acidic solution:
$$NO_3^- (aq) + Ag (s) \rightarrow NO_2 (g) + Ag^+(aq)$$

Oxidation: $Ag (s) \rightarrow Ag^+(aq)$
Reduction: $NO_3^- (aq) \rightarrow NO_2 (g)$

$$e^- + 2 H^+ + NO_3^- (aq) \rightarrow NO_2 (g) + H_2O(l)$$
$$\underline{Ag (s) \rightarrow Ag^+(aq) + e^-}$$
$$2 H^+ + NO_3^- (aq) + Ag (s) \rightarrow NO_2 (g) + H_2O (l) + Ag^+(aq)$$

Balance REDOX in basic solution:
$$MnO_4^-(aq) + HO_2^-(aq) \rightarrow MnO_2(s) + O_2(g)$$

Oxidation: $HO_2^-(aq) \rightarrow O_2(g)$
Reduction: $MnO_4^-(aq) \rightarrow MnO_2(s)$

$$OH^-(aq) + HO_2^-(aq) \rightarrow O_2(g) + H_2O(l) + 2e^-$$
$$3e^- + 2H_2O(l) + MnO_4^-(aq) \rightarrow MnO_2(s) + 4OH^-(aq)$$

Multiply Oxidation Half-Reaction by 3
$$3OH^-(aq) + 3HO_2^-(aq) \rightarrow 3O_2(g) + 3H_2O(l) + 6e^-$$

Multiply Reduction Half-Reaction by 2
$$6e^- + 4 H_2O(l) + 2MnO_4^-(aq) \rightarrow 2MnO_2(s) + 8OH^-(aq)$$
$$H_2O(l) + 2MnO_4^-(aq) + 3HO_2^-(aq) \rightarrow 2MnO_2(s) + 3O_2(g) + 5OH^-(aq)$$

D. Galvanic and Electrolytic cells

1. *Galvanic Cells*—use REDOX reactions to produce an electrical energy flow of electrons.
2. *Salt Bridge*—allows electrons to flow, completing the circuit in the galvanic cell.
3. *Anode*—oxidation will occur, thus producing electrons.
4. *Cathode*—reduction will occur, thus gaining electrons.
5. *Standard Potential/E°*—the measure of the overall potential difference or voltage with all substances at 1.0M concentration.

    i. Calculated $E°$ that is positive favors the product.

    ii. Calculated $E°$ that is negative favors the reactant.

    iii. Gibbs Free Energy relates to $E°$ based on the following equation.

    ‣ $\Delta G°_{rxn} = -nFE$

    ‣ n = number of moles of electrons

    ‣ F = Faradays constant = 9.65×10^4 J/V · mol

    ‣ If $E°$ = a negative number than $\Delta G°_{rxn}$ = positive number, and the reaction is non-spontaneous.

    ‣ If $E°$ = a positive number than $\Delta G°_{rxn}$ = negative number, and the reaction is spontaneous.

Test Tip

*Standard Potentials on the AP test are given in a reference table in the form of reduction potential, or oxidized to reduced. You must switch the sign when writing in the reduced to oxidized form. The more positive the value in the table the better oxidizer it is. In the table on the test, F_2 (g) is the **best** oxidizing agent and therefore is reduced.*

Representation of cell
Zn|Zn²⁺||Cu²⁺|Cu

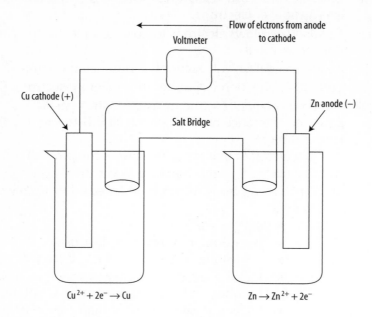

Flow of elctrons from anode to cathode

Voltmeter

Cu cathode (+)

Salt Bridge

Zn anode (−)

$Cu^{2+} + 2e^- \rightarrow Cu$

$Zn \rightarrow Zn^{2+} + 2e^-$

Sample AP Problem

Assume you are constructing a Galvanic cell based on the half reactions between $Zn^{2+}(aq)/Zn(s)$ and $Ag^+(aq)$ /Ag(s). Determine the following:

1. Write a balanced chemical equation and determine $E°$ for the cell.

    i. Based on the table, Zn^{2+} will undertake oxidation, while Ag^+ will undertake reduction.

    ii. Multiply reduction equation by 2 to cancel electrons.

$$Ag^+(aq) + e^- \rightarrow Ag(s) \quad E° = 0.80V$$
$$Zn^{2+}(aq) + 2e^- \rightarrow Zn(s) \quad E° = -0.763V$$

Reduction: $2Ag^+(aq) + 2e^- \rightarrow 2Ag(s) \quad E° = 0.80V$

Oxidation: $Zn(s) \rightarrow Zn^{2+}(aq) + 2e^- \quad E° = +0.763V$ (switch sign)

$2Ag^+(aq) + Zn(s) \rightarrow Zn^{2+}(aq) + 2Ag(s) \quad E° = 1.56V$

2. What is found at cathode and anode?
      i.   Cathode = reduction = $2Ag^+(aq) + 2e^- \rightarrow 2Ag(s)$
      ii. Anode = oxidation = $Zn(s) \rightarrow Zn^{2+}(aq) + 2e^-$
3. Is the reaction product favored or reactant favored?
      i.   Product favored, since the sign for $E°$ is positive.

Test Tip

Galvanic cells are on every AP Chemistry test. Follow the given example as well as the Nernst Equation Example in Chapter 31 and you should be able to handle these questions. In particular, be sure you understand the relationship between Gibbs Free Energy and Standard Potential.

Stoichiometry

I. Stoichiometry

A. Ionic and molecular species present in chemical systems: net ionic equations (see Chapter 11).

B. Balancing of equations, including those for REDOX reactions (see Chapter 11).

1. The relationship of the coefficients between reactants and products in a chemical equation is called stoichiometry.
2. Rules to balance chemical equations.
   i.   The same number and type of atom(s) are both in the reactants and products.
   ii. Coefficients are placed in front of the chemical formula. Do not change the subscripts in the chemical formula.
   iii. All coefficients are in the smallest whole number ratio.
   iv. First balance metals and then non-metals.
   v.   Balance hydrogen and oxygen last.
   vi. Balance polyatomic ions as a unit.
   vii. *Be sure to balance charges.*

Sample AP Problem

What does a chemical equation mean?

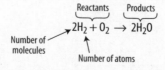

2 molecule of H_2 and 1 molecule O_2 produce 2 molecules H_2O

2 mole of H_2 and 1 mole O_2 produce 2 mole H_2O

Sample Balancing Chemical Equations Questions

(1) $\_\_$ NaI + $\_\_$ Pb(SO$_4$)$_2$ → $\_\_$ PbI$_4$ + $\_\_$ Na$_2$SO$_4$

(2) $\_\_$ VF$_5$ + $\_\_$ HI → $\_\_$ V$_2$I$_{10}$ + $\_\_$ HF

(3) $\_\_$Sr(NO$_3$)$_2$+$\_\_$GaPO$_4$→$\_\_$Sr$_3$(PO$_4$)$_2$+$\_\_$Ga(NO$_3$)$_2$

(4) $\_\_$C$_2$H$_6$+ $\_\_$O$_2$ → $\_\_$CO$_2$+$\_\_$H$_2$O

(5) $\_\_$ Hg$_2$I$_2$ + $\_\_$ O$_2$ → $\_\_$ Hg$_2$O + $\_\_$ I$_2$

Answers

(1)   4,1,1,2

(2)   2,10,1,10

(3)   3,2,1,2

(4)   2,7,4,6*

(5)   2,1,2,2

*For question #4, balance first with fractions and multiply by 2 to make the lowest whole number coefficient.

$$\underline{1}C_2H_6 + \underline{3.5}O_2 \rightarrow \underline{2}CO_2 + \underline{3}H_2O$$

$$\underline{2}C_2H_6 + \underline{7}O_2 \rightarrow \underline{4}CO_2 + \underline{6}H_2O$$

More Difficult Equations to Balance

(1) $\_\_$NH$_3$ + $\_\_$Br$_2$ → $\_\_$N$_2$+$\_\_$NH$_4$$^+$+ $\_\_$Br$^-$

(2) $\_\_$SCl$_2$ + $\_\_$ NH$_3$ → $\_\_$ S$_4$N$_4$+$\_\_$NH$_4$Cl +$\_\_$S

(3) $\_\_$NO + $\_\_$I$^-$ +$\_\_$H → $\_\_$ NH$_4$$^+$+$__I_2$ +$\_\_$H$_2$O

(4) $\_\_$FeCr$_2$O$_4$ + $\_\_$Na$_2$CO$_3$ + $\_\_$O$_2$ → $\_\_$Na$_2$CrO$_4$ +$\_\_$Fe$_2$O$_3$ +$\_\_$ CO$_2$

(1)   8,3,1,6,6

(2)   6,16,1,12,2

(3)   2,10,12,2,5,2

(4)   4,8,7,8,2,8

Stoichiometry Flow Chart

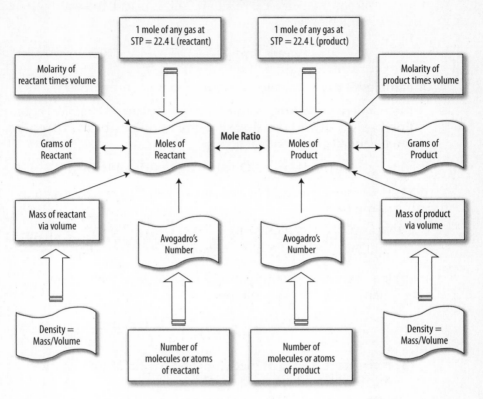

C. Mass and volume relationship with emphasis on the mole concept, including empirical formulas and limiting reactants.

1. *Mole*—represents Avogadro's number (6.022×10^{23}) of atoms or molecules of the pure substance being measured.

2. *Limiting Reagent/Reactant*—the reactant that will be completely used up during the chemical reaction.

3. *Excess Reagent/Reactant*—the reactant that will not be completely used up during the chemical reaction.

4. *Percent Yield*—a method to calculate the effectiveness of a chemical reaction.

   i. Actual Yield—what you produce from actually doing the reaction in a laboratory setting.

ii. Theoretical Yield—what "should have been" produced from the chemical reaction. This is calculated via stoichiometry.

$$Percent\ Yield = \frac{Actual\ Yield}{Theoretical\ Yield} \times 100$$

D. Sample AP Basic Stoichiometry Questions

Methanol is combusted according to the balanced chemical equation below. Answer the stoichiometry questions below based on the balanced chemical reaction.

$$2\ CH_3OH(g) + 3\ O_2(g) \rightarrow 2\ CO_2(g) + 4\ H_2O(g)$$

(1) How many grams of oxygen are required to react with 45 g of methanol?

$$\frac{45\ g\ CH_3OH}{1} \times \frac{1\ mol\ CH_3OH}{32\ g\ CH_3OH} \times \frac{3\ mol\ O_2}{2\ mol\ CH_3OH} \times \frac{32\ g\ O_2}{1\ mol\ O_2} = 68\ g\ O_2$$

(2) If a chemist desires to produce 0.95 mole of water, how many moles of oxygen is needed?

$$\frac{0.95\ mol\ H_2O}{1} \times \frac{3\ mol\ O_2}{4\ mol\ H_2O} = 0.71\ mole\ O_2$$

(3) If you have 34.5 g of methanol and 62.2 g of oxygen, how much water will be produced?

$$\frac{34.5\ g\ CH_3OH}{1} \times \frac{1\ mol\ CH_3OH}{32\ g\ CH_3OH} \times \frac{4\ mol\ H_2O}{2\ mol\ CH_3OH} \times \frac{18\ g\ H_2O}{1\ mol\ H_2O} = 38.8\ g\ H_2O$$

$$\frac{62.2\ g\ O_2}{1} \times \frac{1\ mol\ O_2}{32\ g\ O_2} \times \frac{4\ mol\ H_2O}{3\ mol\ O_2} \times \frac{18\ g\ H_2O}{1\ mol\ H_2O} = 46.7\ g\ H_2O$$

38.8 g H_2O will be produced.

i. Determine the limiting and excess reagent.
   a. Limiting Reagent is CH_3OH
   b. Excessive Reagent is O_2

ii. How much of the excess reagent remains un-reacted?

    a. Since 38.8 g of H_2O is produced, work backwards to find how much O_2 was used.

$$\frac{38.8 \; g \; H_2O}{1} \times \frac{1 \; mol \; H_2O}{18 \; g \; H_2O} \times \frac{3 \; mol \; O_2}{4 \; mol \; H_2O} \times \frac{32 \; g \; O_2}{1 \; mol \; O_2} = 51.7 \; g \; O_2$$

51.7 g O_2 was used

62.2 g O_2 – 51.7g O_2 = 10.5 g O_2 UNUSED or IN EXCESS

iii. When the combustion of methanol was repeated with a chemistry student, 12.4 g of water were produced. What is the percent yield?

$$\text{Percent Yield} = \frac{12.4 \; g \; H_2O}{38.8 \; g \; H_2O} \times 100 = 32.0\%$$

E. Sample AP Solution Stoichiometry Question

Household bleach can be produced based on the chemical reaction below.

2 NaOH (aq) + Cl_2 (g) → NaOCl (aq) + NaCl (aq) + H_2O (l)

(1) What volume of 0.25 M NaOH is required to produce 18 g of NaOCl?

$$\frac{18 \; g \; NaOCl}{1} \times \frac{1 \; mol \; NaOCl}{74.5 \; g \; NaOCl} \times \frac{2 \; mol \; NaOH}{1 \; mol \; NaOCl} \times \frac{1 \; L \; NaOH}{0.25 \; mol \; NaOH} = 1.9 \; L \; NaOH$$

(2) What volume of 0.25 M NaOH is required to react with 0.32 moles of chlorine?

$$\frac{0.32 \; mol \; Cl_2}{1} \times \frac{2 \; mol \; NaOH}{1 \; mol \; Cl_2} \times \frac{1 \; L \; NaOH}{0.25 \; mol \; NaOH} = 2.6 \; L \; NaOH$$

(3) If 4.00 L of 0.25 M NaOH are used with excess chlorine gas, how much NaOCl is produced?

$$\frac{4.00 \; L \; NaOH}{1} \times \frac{0.25 \; mol \; NaOH}{1 \; L \; NaOH} \times \frac{1 \; mol \; NaOCl}{2 \; mol \; NaOH} \times \frac{74.5 \; g \; NaOCl}{1 \; mol \; NaOCl} = 37.3 \; g \; NaOCl$$

F. Sample Calculations Using Density

Liquid bromine is reacted with aluminum to produce aluminum bromide.

$$2\ Al(s) + 3\ Br_2(l) \rightarrow 2AlBr_3(s)$$

If 0.450 L of bromine reacts with excess aluminum, how much aluminum bromide will be made? Density of liquid bromine is 3.1 g/mL.

$$\frac{450\ mL\ Br_2}{1} \times \frac{3.1\ g\ Br_2}{1\ L\ Br_2} \times \frac{1\ mol\ Br_2}{160\ g\ Br_2} \times \frac{1\ mol\ AlBr_3}{3\ mol\ Br_2} \times \frac{27\ g\ AlBr_3}{1\ mol\ AlBr_3} = 776\ g\ AlBr_3$$

Test Tip

Stoichiometry questions can be asked in a multitude of different ways, depending on how the AP test creators want to challenge you. If you use dimensional analysis and your factor label techniques, stoichiometry can actually be a "fun" and easy part of the AP test.

Equilibrium

I. Equilibrium

A. Concept of dynamic equilibrium, physical and chemical.

1. Almost all chemical reactions are reversible.
2. Double arrows indicate reversibility of the reaction ($\rightleftarrows$).
3. Dynamic equilibrium means that the forward and reverse reactions continue at the same rate.

B. Le Chatelier's principle—a change in the factors that govern the chemical equilibrium of a system will cause the system to respond in a manner that counteracts the change.

1. Chemical equilibrium can be disrupted in three different ways.
   i. Change in temperature
   ii. Change in concentration of reactant or product
   iii. Change in volume/pressure.
2. Effect of temperature (will affect the equilibrium constant)
   i. Must know whether the reaction is exothermic or endothermic
      Example—Exothermic:
      $$O_3(g) + O(g) \rightleftarrows 2O_2(g) \quad \Delta H = -318 \text{ kJ}$$

      Rewrite the equation as follows:
      $$O_3(g) + O(g) \rightleftarrows 2O_2(g) + 318 \text{ kJ}$$

      ▸ If heat is "added" to the system, the result would favor the formation of the reactants or the endothermic reaction.

> ▸ If heat is "taken away" from the system, the result would favor the formation of the products or the exothermic reaction.

Example—Endothermic:

$$2HCl(g) \rightleftarrows H_2(g)+Cl_2(g) \; \Delta H=185 \; kJ$$

Rewrite the equation as follows:
$$185 \; kJ+ 2HCl(g) \rightleftarrows H_2(g)+Cl_2(g)$$

> ▸ If heat is "added" to the system, the result would favor the formation of the products or the endothermic reaction.
> ▸ If heat is "taken away" from the system, the result would favor the formation of the reactants or the exothermic reaction.

3. Effect of concentration change (no effect on equilibrium constant).

Example—$N_2(g)+3H_2(g) \rightleftarrows 2NH_3(g)$

> ▸ If the concentration of the reactant(s) is decreased, the result would favor the formation of the reactants.
> ▸ If the concentration of the reactant(s) is increased, the result would favor the formation of the products.
> ▸ If the concentration of the product is decreased, the result would favor the formation of the products.
> ▸ If the concentration of the product is increased, the result would favor the formation of the reactants.

4. Effect of volume/pressure change (no effect on equilibrium constant)

  i. Must count the number of gas molecules of reactants and products to accurately predict the direction.

   Example—$2NO_2(g) \rightleftarrows N_2O_4(g)$

   2 gas molecules of reactant—1 gas molecule of product

> ▸ If the volume increases (pressure decreases), the system will shift to the side with the greatest number of gas molecules or reactants in the example above.

> ▸ If the volume decreases (pressure increases), the system will shift to the side with the least number of gas molecules or product in the example above.

Sample AP Question

Based on the following reaction, predict whether products or reactants are favored when the following stresses are applied to the system.

$$aA(g)+bB(g) \rightleftarrows cC(g) \; \Delta H = +$$

   i.   Decrease in temperature—Favor reactants
   ii.   Increase in pressure—Favor products
   iii.   Decrease in volume—same as increase in pressure—Favor products
   iv.   Add more reactant *A*—Favor products
   v.   Add a catalyst—No change

C. Quantitative treatment
   1. Equilibrium constants for gaseous reactions: *Kp, Kc*
      i.   Equilibrium constant relates the concentrations of reactants and products at equilibrium for a given temperature.

         For the general reaction: $aA + bB \rightleftarrows cC + dD$

$$\text{Equilibrium constant} = K = \frac{[C]^c [D]^d}{[A]^a [B]^b}$$

> ▸ Molar product concentrations are in the numerator.
> ▸ Molar reactant concentrations are in the denominator.
> ▸ Each concentration is raised to the power of the stoichiometric coefficient.
> ▸ Pure solids, pure liquids, and water are not placed into the expression.
> ▸ The expression K_c indicates that C (concentrations) are being measured in moles per liter.

▶ The expression K_p indicates that P (partial pressures) are being measured in pressure units.

▶ The value of K is independent of concentration.

Examples

1. $N_2(g)+3H_2(g) \rightleftarrows 2NH_3(g)$

$$K_c = \frac{[NH_3]^2}{[N_2][H_2]^3} \qquad K_p = \frac{P^2_{NH_3}}{P_{N_2}P^3_{H_2}}$$

2. $2KClO_3\ (s) \rightleftarrows 2KCl(s)+3O_2(g)$

$$K_c = [O_2]^3 \qquad\qquad K_p = P^3_{O_2}$$

3. $NH_3(aq)+H_2O(l) \rightleftarrows NH_4^+(aq)+OH^-(aq)$

$$K_C = \frac{[NH_4^+][OH^-]}{[NH_3]}$$

D. Manipulation of the Equilibrium Constant

1. Multiplying a chemical equation by a coefficient

Example:

$A(s) + \dfrac{1}{2}B_2(g) \rightleftarrows AB(g)\ K = 2.3 \times 10^3$

If the equation above is multiplied by 2, the value of K is squared:

$2A(s) + B_2(g) \rightleftarrows 2AB(g)\ K = 5.29 \times 10^6$

Rule: If the balanced chemical equation is multiplied by a factor, the value of K is raised to that power.

2. Reversing the reaction

Hypothetical Example:

$A(s) + B\ (g) \rightleftarrows AB(g)\ K = 4.0 \times 10^3$

If the equation above is reversed, the value K is the reciprocal of the original K:

$AB(g) \rightleftarrows A(s) +B(g)\ K = 2.5 \times 10^{-4}$

Rule: If the balanced chemical equation is reversed, the new value of K can be expressed in the following way:

$K_{new} = 1/K_{original}$

3. When several equations are used to obtain a net balanced chemical equation, then $K_{total} = K_1 \cdot K_2 \cdot K_3$.

    Equation 1: C (graphite) + $1/2O_2(g) \rightleftarrows CO(g)$ $K = 2.28 \times 10^{23}$
    Equation 2: C (graphite) + $O_2(g) \rightleftarrows CO_2(g)$ $K = 1.25 \times 10^{69}$

    What is the equilibrium constant for the following reaction?
    $$2CO(g) + O_2(g) \rightleftarrows 2CO_2(g)$$

    ▸ Equation 1: Reverse and multiply by 2
    $2CO(g) \rightleftarrows 2C(graphite) + O_2(g)$ $K = 1.92 \times 10^{-47}$
    ▸ Equation 2: Multiply by 2
    $2C$ (graphite) + $2O_2(g) \rightleftarrows 2CO_2(g)$ $K = 1.56 \times 10^{138}$
    ▸ Multiply both K for both equations: 3.00×10^{91}

E. What does the equilibrium constant mean?

1. If $K > 1$, then the product formation is favored—equilibrium concentrations of products are greater.
2. If $K < 1$, then the reaction formation is favored—equilibrium concentrations of reactants are greater.
3. If $K = 1$, the concentrations of reactants and products are equal.

F. Reaction Quotient

1. A measure of the proportions of the products to reactants in a chemical equation.
2. Not always a measure at equilibrium, but can be.
    $$aA + bB \rightarrow cC + dD$$

    $$Q = \text{reaction quotient} = \frac{[C]^c[D]^d}{[A]^a[B]^b}$$

    i.   If $Q < K$, the system is not at equilibrium and product formation is favored.
    ii. If $Q > K$, the system is not at equilibrium and the reactant formation is favored.
    iii. If $Q = K$, the reaction is at equilibrium.

Sample AP Problems

Problem 1: Equilibrium Concentrations are given

A mixture of HI, H_2, and I_2 gases are in a reaction vessel and allowed to reach equilibrium at a temperature of 723K. The equilibrium concentrations for each are listed below. Calculate the K or K_c for the reaction.

$$[HI] = 2.50 \times 10^{-2}M, \; [H_2] = 6.33 \times 10^{-4}M, \; [I_2] = 1.23 \times 10^{-3}M$$

$$2\,HI\,(g) \leftrightarrow H_2(g) + I_2(g)$$

$$K_c = \frac{[H_2][I_2]}{[HI]^2} = \frac{[6.33 \times 10^{-4}][1.23 \times 10^{-3}]}{[2.50 \times 10^{-2}]^2} = 1.25 \times 10^{-3}$$

Problem 2: Equilibrium Concentrations are not given

1.00 mol of H_2 and 1.00 mol of S_2 are placed in a 1.00L flask at 900K. When equilibrium is achieved, 0.750 mol of H_2S has formed. Calculate K_c, at 900K for the reaction below.

$$2H_2(g) + S_2(g) \leftrightarrow 2\,H_2S\,(g)$$

Equation	$2H_2$	S_2	$2H_2S$
Initial moles	1.00	1.00	0
Change	−0.750	$\dfrac{-0.750}{2}$	+0.750
Equilibrium moles	1.00−0.750	$1-\dfrac{0.750}{2}$	0.750
Concentration at Equilibrium	0.25	0.625	0.750

$$K_c = \frac{[H_2S]^2}{[H_2]^2[S_2]} = \frac{[0.750]^2}{[.25]^2[0.625]} = 14.4$$

G. Constants for acids and bases; pK; pH

1. Acid—equilibrium constant (pK_a)

$$HA(aq) + H_2O(l) \rightleftarrows H_3O^+ (aq) + A^-(aq)$$

$$K_a = \frac{[H_3O^+][A^-]}{[HA]}$$

$$pK_a = -logK_a$$

   i. Strong acids have large K_a values since they produce high amounts of product (hydronium) as a result of a higher amount of dissociation.
   ii. Weak acids have small K_a values since they produce small amounts of product (hydronium) as a result of a smaller amount of dissociation.

2. Base—equilibrium constant (pK_b)

$$B(aq) + H_2O(l) \rightleftarrows BH^+ (aq) + OH^-(aq)$$

$$K_b = \frac{[BH^+][OH^-]}{[B]}$$

$$pK_b = -logK_b$$

   i. Strong bases have large K_b values since they produce high amounts of product (hydroxide) as a result of a higher amount of dissociation.
   ii. Weak bases have small K_b values since they produce small amounts of product (hydroxide) as a result of a smaller amount of dissociation.

3. Water—Ionization Constant (K_w)

$$2H_2O(l) \rightleftarrows H_3O^+(aq) + OH^-(aq)$$

$$K_w = [H_3O^+][OH^-] = 1 \times 10^{-14} \text{ at } 25°C$$

$$K_a \cdot K_b = K_w$$

4. pH and pOH-based on powers of ten.
   i. pH—measure of hydronium concentration

$$pH = -log[H_3O^+]$$

   ii. pOH—measure of hydroxide concentration

$$pOH = -log[OH^-]$$

$$pH + pOH = 14$$

5. Polyprotic acids
   i.   Capable of donating more than one proton.
   ii. K_a values become smaller after each successive step, meaning it is more difficult to remove a proton each time.
   iii. pH of a polyprotic acid depends on the first ionization step.

Sample AP Questions

1. Calculate the following when 0.32 g of LiOH is dissolved in 234 mL of water?

   $$0.32 \ g \ LiOH = 0.013 \ mol \ LiOH = \frac{0.013 \ mol}{0.234 \ L} = 0.056 \ M$$

   a. Hydroxide Concentration
      LiOH is a strong base and therefore dissociates completely.
      $[OH^-] = 0.056 \ M$
   b. Hydronium Concentration
      $K_w = [H_3O^+][OH^-] = 1 \times 10^{-14}$
      $1 \times 10^{-14} = [H_3O^+][0.056]$
      $[H_3O^+] = 1.79 \times 10^{-13} \ M$
   c. pH
      $pH = -log[H_3O^+]$
      $pH = -log[1.79 \times 10^{-13}] = 12.75$
   d. pOH
      $pH + pOH = 14$
      $12.75 + pOH = 14$
      $pOH = 1.25$

2. If the pH of a solution is 8.39 find the following:
   a. Hydronium Concentration
      $pH = -log[H_3O^+]$
      $8.39 = -log[H_3O^+]$
      $10^{-8.39} = 4.07 \times 10^{-9}$
   b. Hydroxide Concentration
      $K_w = [H_3O^+][OH^-] = 1 \times 10^{-14}$
      $1 \times 10^{-14} = [OH^-][4.07 \times 10^{-9}]$
      $[OH^-] = 2.46 \times 10^{-6}$
   c. pOH
      $pOH = 5.61$

3. What is the hydronium concentration in 0.25 M HNO_2 ($K_a = 4.5 \times 10^{-4}$)?

$$HNO_2(aq) \rightleftarrows H^+ (aq) + NO_2^- (aq) \text{ (monoprotic acid)}$$

$$K_a = \frac{[H_3O^+][NO_2^-]}{[HNO_2]}$$

$$4.5 \times 10^{-4} = \frac{[x][x]}{[0.25]} = \frac{x^2}{0.25}$$

$$x = 1.1 \times 10^{-2} = [HNO_2]$$

4. If the acid dissociation constant, K_a, for an acid HA is 3.2×10^{-4} at 25 °C, what percent of the acid is dissociated in a 0.30-molar solution of HA at 25°C?

$$HA(aq) \rightleftarrows H^+(aq) + A^-(aq)$$

$$K_a = \frac{[H^+][A^-]}{[HA]}$$

$$3.2 \times 10^{-4} = \frac{[x][x]}{[0.30]} = \frac{x^2}{0.30}$$

$$x = 9.7 \times 10^{-3} = [HA]$$

$$Percent\ ionized = \frac{quantity\ of\ acid\ ionized}{initial\ acid\ concentration} \times 100 = \frac{9.7 \times 10^{-3}}{0.30} \times 100 = 3.2\%$$

5. A 0.15-molar solution of a weak monoprotic acid, HA, has a pH of 3.00. Determine the ionization constant of this acid.

$$pH = 3.00 [H_3O^+] = 1 \times 10^{-3}\ M$$

$$HA(aq) \rightleftarrows H^+(aq) + A^-(aq)$$

$$K_a = \frac{[H^+][A^-]}{[HA]}$$

$$K_a = \frac{[1 \times 10^{-3}][1 \times 10^{-3}]}{[0.15]} = 6.7 \times 10^{-6}$$

H. Solubility product constants and their application to precipitation and the dissolution of slightly soluble compounds

1. Solubility product constant or K_{sp}, is defined as the product of the two concentrations that dissolve in the reaction.

2. Does not measure the solubility of a compound, but, in general, the smaller the K_{sp}, the less soluble the compound.

For the general reaction:

$$A_xB_y(s) \rightleftarrows xA^{y+}(aq) + yB^{x-}(aq)$$
$$K_{sp} = [A^{y+}]^x[B^{x-}]^y$$

Examples:

$$PbCl_2(s) \rightleftarrows Pb^{2+}(aq) + 2Cl^-(aq) \qquad K_{sp} = [Pb^{2+}][Cl^-]^2$$

$$AgI(s) \rightleftarrows Ag^+(aq) + I^-(aq) \qquad K_{sp} = [Ag^+][I^-]$$

Sample AP Questions

1. The solubility of $AgBr$ is 5.74×10^{-7} mol/L at 25°C. Calculate the K_{sp} of $AgBr$.

$$AgBr(s) \rightleftarrows Ag^+(aq) + Br^-(aq)$$

$$K_{sp} = [Ag^+][Br^-]$$

$$K_{sp} = [5.74 \times 10^{-7}] [5.74 \times 10^{-7}] = 3.29 \times 10^{-13}$$

2. Calcium fluoride will dissolve in water. If the concentration of Ca^{2+} is 1.34×10^{-2} M find the K_{sp} for calcium fluoride.

$$CaF_2(s) \rightleftarrows Ca^{2+}(aq) + 2F^-(aq)$$

$$K_{sp} = [Ca^{2+}][2F^-]^2$$

$$K_{sp} = [1.34 \times 10^{-2}] [2 \cdot 1.34 \times 10^{-2}]^2 = 9.62 \times 10^{-6}$$

3. If the K_{sp} for BaF_2 is 1.7×10^{-6} determine the concentration of the salt.

$$BaF_2(s) \rightleftarrows Ba^{2+}(aq) + 2F^-(aq)$$

$$K_{sp} = [x][2x]^2$$

$$1.7 \times 10^{-6} = 4x^3$$

$$x = 7.5 \times 10^{-3} \text{ M } BaF_2$$

I. Solubility Product and Reaction Quotient Q

1. If $Q = K_{sp}$, the system is at equilibrium—no more solute will dissolve because the solution is saturated.

2. If $Q < K_{sp}$ the system is not at equilibrium, the solution is not saturated, and more solute can dissolve.

3. If $Q > K_{sp}$ the system is not at equilibrium, the solution is supersaturated, and solute will precipitate.

J. *Common Ion Effect*—two different sources of the same ion are involved in a specific equilibrium reaction.

Test Tip

Be prepared!!! *Remember that the first question in the free-response section of the exam will ask about equilibrium. As you review this chapter, practice the problems in Chapter 30. By doing so, you'll be more than ready for this question.*

Kinetics

I. Kinetics

A. Concept of rate of reaction

1. *Rate of a Chemical Reaction*—changes in concentration or pressure of a substance per unit of time.
2. Can be measured as the decrease of the reactant per unit of time.
3. Can be measured as the increase of the product per unit of time.

B. Conditions that can affect rate

1. *Temperature*—increase in temperature usually results in a faster reaction.
2. *Catalyst*—increase rate by lowering the activation energy of a reaction.
3. *Concentration of Reactants*—increases the amount of reactants colliding with each other, thus yielding product.
4. *Surface Area*—increasing the surface area of the reactant can increase the rate.

C. Use of experimental data and graphical analysis to determine reactant order, rate constants, and reaction rate laws.

Decomposition of hydrogen peroxide

$$2H_2O_2(aq) \rightleftarrows 2H_2O(l) + O_2(g)$$

Rate of the reaction is proportional to the concentration of H_2O_2

Rate of reaction = $k[H_2O_2]$

where k is the rate constant

1. General formula for rate equation

$$aA + bB \xrightarrow{s} dD$$

$$Rate\ of\ reaction = k[A]^x\ k[B]^y\ k[C]^z$$

^{x}, ^{y}, ^{z} are *not* necessarily stoichiometric coefficients

2. Rate Order
   i. The order of a reactant is the exponent of the concentration term.

$$2H_2O_2(aq) \rightleftarrows 2H_2O(l) + O_2(g)$$

$$Rate\ of\ reaction = k[H_2O_2]$$

   The reaction is first order with respect to the reactant H_2O_2.

   ii. Determining Rate Order

$$2NO(g) + Cl_2(g) \rightleftarrows 2NOCl(g)$$

$$Rate\ of\ reaction = k[NO]^2[Cl_2]$$

   The reaction is second order with respect to NO and first order with respect to Cl_2 and third order overall.

Trial	[NO] mol/L	[Cl_2] mol/L	Rate
1	0.200	0.200	1.20×10^{-6}
2	0.400	0.200	4.80×10^{-6}
3	0.200	0.400	2.40×10^{-6}
4	0.400	0.400	9.6×10^{-6}

▸ Trial 1—gives the reaction rate when both concentrations are the same.
▸ Trial 2—if the concentration of NO is doubled, the reaction rate is increased 4 times since NO is second order ($2^2 = 4$).
▸ Trial 3—if the concentration of Cl_2 is doubled, then the reaction rate is doubled since Cl_2 is first order ($2^1 = 2$).
▸ Trial 4—both reactants are doubled, therefore the rate is 8 times the value ($2^3 = 8$).

Sample AP Question

Based on the data below, determine the rate equation for the reaction and the rate constant.

Trial	[A] mol/L	[B] mol/L	Rate
1	2.1×10^{-3}	1.2×10^{-3}	5.6×10^{-6}
2	2.1×10^{-3}	2.4×10^{-3}	11.2×10^{-6}
3	2.1×10^{-3}	0.6×10^{-3}	2.80×10^{-6}
4	4.2×10^{-3}	1.2×10^{-3}	11.2×10^{-6}
5	6.3×10^{-3}	1.2×10^{-3}	16.8×10^{-6}

- ▸ Trials 1–3 show that the rate increases by 2 (trial 1 and 2) or decreases by ½ (trials 1 and 3). This indicates first order to reactant B.
- ▸ Trials 1, 4, and 5 show that the rate doubles and triples in 4 and 5 when compared to trial 1. This indicates first order with respect to reactant A.

$$Rate\ of\ reaction = k[A][B]$$
$$5.6 \times 10^{-6} = k(2.1 \times 10^{-3})(1.2 \times 10^{-3})$$
$$k = 2.22$$

iii. Zero Order Rate Reaction
  - ▸ The rate of the reaction is independent of the concentration of the reactant(s).
  - ▸ *Rate = k*

iv. First Order Rate Reaction
  - ▸ The rate of the reaction is directly proportional to the concentration of one of the reactants.
  - ▸ *Rate = k[A]*

v. Second Order Rate Reaction
  - ▸ The rate of the reaction is directly proportional to the square of the concentration of one of the reactants.
  - ▸ *Rate = k[A]²*

vi. Using Data to Uncover Order

Order	Rate Law	Straight Line Plot
0	$Rate = k$	$[A]$ versus T
1	$Rate = k[A]$	$ln[A]$ versus T
2	$Rate = k[A]^2$	$\dfrac{1}{[A]}$ versus T

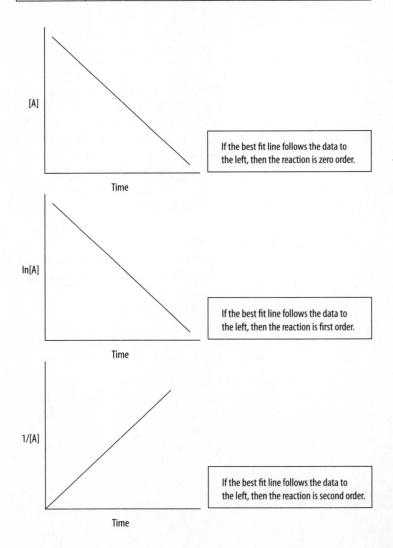

If the best fit line follows the data to the left, then the reaction is zero order.

If the best fit line follows the data to the left, then the reaction is first order.

If the best fit line follows the data to the left, then the reaction is second order.

D. Effect of temperature change on rates, energy of activation, and the role of catalysts

1. Collision Theory—fundamental conditions for reactions to occur.
   i. Reacting molecules must collide with each other.
   ii. Reacting molecules must collide with sufficient energy.
   iii. Reacting molecules must collide such that a rearrangement of atoms can occur.
2. Activation Energy—energy required to get a reaction to go to products.
   i. Catalyst will lower the activation energy without being consumed in the chemical reaction.
3. Effect of Temperature
   i. A rise in temperature will increase kinetic energy, thus allowing more collisions between reactants. The net result is to increase the rate of the reaction.

E. The relationship between the rate-determining step and a mechanism

1. Reaction Mechanism—the sequence of bond breaking and bond making steps that lead to an overall chemical reaction. Each individual step is called an elementary step.
2. If 1 reactant is involved in an elementary step, it is called unimolecular.
3. If 2 reactants are involved in an elementary step, it is called bimolecular.
4. The rate of reaction for an elementary step is based on the stoichiometric coefficient. This is different from experimentally determining the rate and order of a reaction.
5. The slowest elementary step is called the rate-determining step (rate limiting). The overall order and rate of the reaction will be the same as the slowest or rate-determining step.

   For the overall reaction of: $2\ NO_2 + F_2 \rightleftarrows 2\ NO_2F$

   $$NO_2 + F_2 \rightleftarrows NO_2F + F \text{ (slow)}$$
   $$NO_2 + F \rightleftarrows NO_2F \text{ (fast)}$$

In the slow rate-determining step, the rate equation is the following:

$$Rate = k[NO_2][F_2] \text{ or second order}$$

EXPERIMENTALLY the rate for $2\ NO_2 + F_2 \rightleftharpoons 2\ NO_2F$ is second order

(same as slow rate-determining step)

Determining the order of a chemical reaction is a fundamental principle that all released AP exams have had. Free-response questions frequently require students to know the laws of kinetics. For examples, see the AP Chemistry released exams at the College Board website.

Thermodynamics

I. Thermodynamics

A. *Temperature*—measure of the average kinetic energy of a substance.

B. *Heat*—transfer of energy from one object to another.

C. State functions

1. A quantity determined independent of the path chosen.
2. State functions include: enthalpy, entropy, and free energy.

D. First law: change in enthalpy; heat of formation; heat of reaction; Hess's law; heat of vaporization and heat of fusion; calorimetry.

1. *First Law of Thermodynamics*—energy cannot be created or destroyed, but can only be changed from one form to another.
2. *Specific Heat Capacity*—defined as the heat required that will result in a temperature change per one gram of a substance. Metals have a low specific heat, indicating less energy is required to raise their temperature. As a comparison, water has a relatively high specific heat.

$$\text{Specific Heat Capacity } (C_p) = \frac{\text{quantity of heat supplied}}{\text{(mass of object) (temperature change)}}$$

Substance	Specific Heat $(J/g \cdot K)$
Al	0.902
Water (l)	4.184
Glass	0.84

3. Measuring the amount of heat transferred can be calculated using the equation below:

$$q = (m)(C_p)(\Delta T)$$
$$q = \text{heat transferred}$$
$$m = \text{mass of substance}$$
$$C_p = \text{specific heat}$$
$$\Delta T = T_f - T_i = \text{change in temperature}$$

ΔT object	Sign of ΔT	Sign of q	Direction of Heat Transfer
Increase	+	+	Heat transferred into object
Decrease	−	−	Heat transferred out of object

Sample AP Question

A 21.3 g sample of a metal is heated to 70°C and dropped into 62.4 g of water at 21°C. The final temperature of water is 24°C. Find the specific heat of the metal.

$$q_{water} = q = (mass)(C_p)(\Delta T)$$

$$q_{water} = (62.4\ g)(4.184 \frac{J}{g} \cdot °C)(24°C - 21°C)$$

$$q_{water} = 783\ J$$

Since heat was transferred from the metal to the water:

$$q_{water} = {}^-q_{metal}$$

$${}^-q_{metal} = q = (mass)(C_p)(\Delta T)$$

$$-783\ J = (21.3\ g)\ (C_p)(24°C - 70°C)$$

$$(C_p) = 0.799 \frac{J}{g} \cdot °C$$

4. *Heating Curve*—graphical depiction of the changes of state for a particular substance as heat is added to it.

   ▸ *Heat of Fusion*—amount of heat required to melt a substance. Note that when melting takes place, the temperature is constant.

> ‣ *Heat of Vaporization*—amount of heat required to boil or evaporate a substance. Note when boiling takes place the temperature is constant.

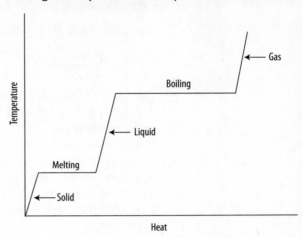

5. *Enthalpy*—heat transferred into or out of a system. Also called ΔH. Measured in kJ/mol.
> ‣ *System*—refers to the substances undergoing a reaction
> ‣ *Surroundings*—everything that is outside of the system
> ‣ *Endothermic*—energy transferred from the surroundings to the system
> ‣ *Exothermic*—energy transferred from the system to the surroundings

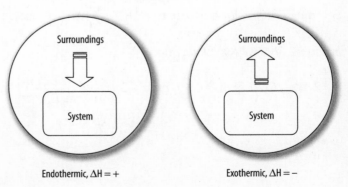

$$\Delta H = H_{products} - H_{reactants}$$

Sample AP Question

Based on the equation below, how much heat is produced by the decomposition of 56.4 g of $C_2H_5OH(l)$?

$$C_2H_5OH(l) \rightarrow 2\ C(graphite) + 3\ H_2(l) + 0.5\ O_2(g) \quad H = 228\ kJ/mol$$

$$\frac{56.4\ g\ C_2H_5OH}{1} \times \frac{1\ mol\ C_2H_5OH}{46\ g\ C_2H_5OH} \times \frac{228\ kJ}{1\ mol\ C_2H_5OH} = 280\ kJ$$

▸ *Standard Enthalpies of Formation*—amount of energy required to form 1 mole of a substance from its elements. Also called ΔH_f°. Elements have a value of zero.

▸ *Standard Enthalpy of a Reaction*—when a reaction occurs with all products and reactants in a standard state. Also called ΔH°. Superscript indicates standard conditions of 25°C and 1 barr of pressure.

Enthalpy Change for a Reaction $= \Delta H_{rxn}^\circ = \sum \left[\Delta H_f^\circ (products) \right] - \sum \left[\Delta H_f^\circ (reactants) \right]$

Sample AP Question

What is the standard enthalpy change, ΔH_{rxn}°. for the reaction below? The enthalpies of formation: $CH_4 - 75$ kJ/mol, $CO_2 - 394$ kJ/mol, and $H_2O(l) - 286$ kJ/mol.

$$CH_4 + 2\ O_2 \rightarrow CO_2 + 2\ H_2O$$

Enthalpy Change for a Reaction $= \Delta H_{rxn}^\circ = \sum \left[\Delta H_f^\circ (products) \right] - \sum \left[\Delta H_f^\circ (reactants) \right]$

Enthalpy Change for a Reaction $= \Delta H_{rxn}^\circ$

$$\sum \left[2\ mole\ H_2O \left(-286\ \frac{kJ}{mol} \right) + 1\ mole\ CO_2 \left(-394\ \frac{kJ}{mol} \right) \right] - \sum \left[1\ mole\ CH_4 \left(-75\ \frac{kJ}{mol} \right) \right]$$

$$= -891\ kJ$$

> ▸ *Hess's Law*—the overall enthalpy of a reaction is the sum of all the reactions for the process

i. Rule 1: If you reverse the reactions, change the sign of ΔH.

$A + B \rightarrow C \qquad \Delta H = 60$ kJ

$C \rightarrow A + B \qquad \Delta H = -60$ kJ

ii. Rule 2: If you multiply the reaction by a coefficient, multiply the value of ΔH by the coefficient.

$A + B \rightarrow C \qquad \Delta H = 60$ kJ

$2A + 2B \rightarrow 2C \qquad \Delta H = 120$ kJ

iii. Rule 1 and 2 can be combined.

$A + B \rightarrow C \qquad \Delta H = 60$ kJ

$3C \rightarrow 3A + 3B \qquad \Delta H = -180$ kJ

Sample AP Problem

Use the equations in 2 and 3 below to determine the enthalpy for the reaction for equation 1.

Equation 1: $4PCl_3(g) \rightarrow P_4(s) + 6Cl_2(g)$

Equation 2: $P_4(s) + 10Cl_2(g) \rightarrow 4PCl_5(g) \quad \Delta H = 813$ kJ

Equation 3: $PCl_3(g) + Cl_2(g) \rightarrow PCl_5(g) \quad \Delta H = 1146$ kJ

> ▸ Reverse equation 2:
> $4PCl_5(g) \rightarrow P_4(s) + 10Cl_2(g) \quad \Delta H = -813$ kJ
> ▸ Multiply equation 3 by 4:
> $4PCl_3(g) + 4Cl_2(g) \rightarrow 4PCl_5(g) \; \Delta H = 4584$ kJ
> ▸ Sum equations and cancel
> $4PCl_3(g) \rightarrow P_4(s) + 6Cl_2(g) \quad \Delta H = 3771$ kJ
> ▸ *Calorimetry*—measuring the heat of a chemical reaction using a calorimeter

▶ Coffee Cup Calorimeter—Styrofoam cups can be used as insulators to measure temperature changes without a loss to the surroundings.

Use $q = (mass)(C_p)(\Delta T)$

Sample AP Question

2.00g of metal (specific heat=0.3 J/g·°C) are added to a coffee cup calorimeter that contains 100.0 mL of water. The temperature rises from 32°C to 34°C. Determine the enthalpy change for the reaction per gram.

$$q = (mass)(C_p)(\Delta T)$$

$$q = (102.0g)\left(0.3\frac{J}{g}\cdot {}^{\circ}C\right)(2{}^{\circ}C) = 61.2\,J = 30.6\frac{J}{g}$$

E. Second law: entropy; free energy of formation; free energy of reaction; dependence of change in free energy on enthalpy and entropy changes.

1. *Second Law of Thermodynamics*—entropy or disorder of the universe will increase over time.

2. *Entropy*—measurement of disorder. Also call ΔS. Measured in J/K · mol.

   ▶ Entropies of gases are larger than liquids, and liquid entropies are larger than solids.

▸ Entropies are greater for more complex molecules.

Entropy Change for a system =

$$\Delta S^\circ_{system} = \sum \left[S^\circ (products) \right] - \sum \left[S^\circ (reactants) \right]$$

▸ If ΔS°_{system} is negative, then less products are formed and less disorder.

▸ If ΔS°_{system} is positive, then more products are formed and more disorder.

3. *Standard Free Energies of Formation*—amount of free energy required to form 1 mole of a substance from its elements. Also called ΔG°_f. Elements have a value of zero.

4. *Gibbs Free Energy*—the amount of energy in a reaction that can be used for work.

   ▸ If $\Delta G > 0$ the reaction is non-spontaneous and energy must be added to the reaction for it to occur. Reaction formation is favored.

   ▸ If $\Delta G < 0$ the reaction is spontaneous and no outside source of energy needs to be added. Product formation is favored.

   ▸ If $\Delta G = 0$ the reaction is at equilibrium.

   Free Energy Change for a reaction =

   $$\Delta G^\circ_{reaction} = \sum \left[\Delta G^\circ_f (products) \right] - \sum \left[\Delta G^\circ_f (reactants) \right]$$

   $$\Delta G^\circ_{system} = \Delta H^\circ_{system} - T \Delta S$$

5. Determining a Reaction as Product or Reactant Favored

   Based on the table of values below for the following reaction, determine ΔH, ΔS, ΔG.

$$H_2S(g) + 2O_2(g) \rightleftarrows H_2SO_4(l)$$

	H_2S	O_2	H_2SO_4
$\Delta H^\circ_f (kJ/mol)$	−20	0	−814
$\Delta S (J/K \cdot mol)$	206	205	157
$\Delta G^\circ_f (kJ/mol)$	−34	0	−690

▸ $\Delta H_f^\circ = [1(-814)] - [1(-20)] = -794$ *kJ/mol*
▸ $\Delta S = [1(157)] - [1(206) + 2(205)] = -459$ *J/K · mol*
▸ $\Delta G_f^\circ = [1(-690)] - [1(-34)] = -656$ *kJ/mol*
If ΔG is negative the product is favored.

6. Relationship between ΔH, ΔS, ΔG

Sign of ΔH	Sign of ΔS	Sign of $-T\Delta S$	Sign of ΔG
(−)	(+)	(−)	− spontaneous
(−)	(−)	(+)	− at low temp (spontaneous) + at high temp (non-spontaneous)
(+)	(+)	(−)	+ at low temp (non-spontaneous) − at high temp (spontaneous)
(+)	(−)	(+)	+ non-spontaneous

F. Relationship of change in free energy to equilibrium constants

1. Gibbs Free Energy can be calculated under non-standard conditions.

$\Delta G^\circ = -RTlnK$

   R = *ideal gas law constant*
   T = *temperature in Kelvin*
   K = *equilibrium constant*

G. Catalyst

1. A catalyst works by lowering the activation energy (E_a) of a reaction. *Activation energy* is defined as the amount of input energy needed to start a chemical reaction.

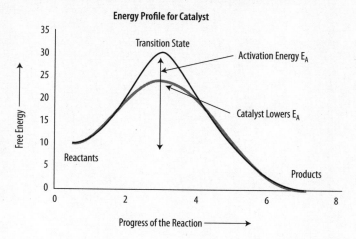

Energy Profile for Catalyst

- Transition State
- Activation Energy E_A
- Catalyst Lowers E_A
- Reactants
- Products

Free Energy →

Progress of the Reaction →

Test Tip

Expect to have enthalpy, entropy, and free energy asked about in combination with each other. Be sure you understand the relationships between thermodynamic concepts for the AP Chemistry exam.

PART V:

DESCRIPTIVE CHEMISTRY

Chemical Reactivity

I. Chemical Reactivity

A. Facts to Know

1. A large portion of the AP Chemistry exam revolves around the ability to write and chemically balance chemical equations.

2. Color changes of ions and compounds are quite common on the test.

Ion	Color
Cu	Greenish blue
Fe	Red-orange rust color
Co	Pink/Red
Ni	Green
Cr	Green
CrO_4^{2-} (chromate)	Yellow
$Cr_2O_7^{2-}$ (dichromate)	Orange

Compound	Color
NO_2	Brown gas
PbI_2	Yellow
AgCl	White
Insoluble Barium	White
AgI	Yellow
$KMnO_4$ (potassium permanganate)	Purple

II. Example Reactions with High Probability on the Exam

A. Metal with Reactive Gases.

1. Metals such as Pb, Fe, Cu, Sn, K, Na, Al.
2. Gases include fluorine, oxygen, chlorine (all diatomic).
3. The metal assumes the highest possible charge when reacting with the gas. These metals would include Fe, Cu, Sn, Pb.
4. Charges of ions to know: Fe^{2+}, Fe^{3+}, Sn^{2+}, Sn^{4+}, Pb^{2+}, Pb^{4+}, Cu^+, Cu^{2+}

   A sample of tin metal is heated with chlorine gas.
   i. Balanced Equation
      ▸ $Sn + 2Cl_2 \rightarrow SnCl_4$

B. Formation of an acid from non-metallic oxide.

1. A synthesis reaction
   Sulfur trioxide is reacted with water vapor.
   i. Balanced Equation
      ▸ $SO_3 + H_2O \rightarrow H_2SO_4$

C. Replacement of halogen with a more reactive halogen.

1. Reactivity of halogens: $F_2 > Cl_2 > Br_2 > I_2$.
2. Spectator ions should not be written.
3. Balance charges as well as atoms.
   Chlorine gas is bubbled into a solution of sodium iodide.
   i. Balanced Equation
      ▸ $Cl_2 + 2I^- \rightarrow 2Cl^- + I_2$
   Note: Sodium is a spectator and *not* written in the reaction.

D. Halogens (Cl and Br) with Hydroxide Ion

   1. Hypohalite ion is formed.
   2. ClO^- (hypochlorite) , BrO^- (hyprobromite) are 2 main hypohalites.

      Free bromine is added to dilute sodium hydroxide.

      i. Balanced Equation

          ▸ $Br_2 + 2OH^- \rightarrow Br^- + BrO^- + H_2O$

E. Replacement of a metal with a more active metal.

   1. The metal assumes the highest possible charge when reacting with the gas.

      Zinc metal is immersed in a solution of silver nitrate.

      i. Balanced Equation

          ▸ $Zn + 2Ag^+ \rightarrow Zn^{2+} + 2Ag$

F. Oxides of Group 1 and 2 with water

   1. Hydroxides will form
   2. Exothermic reaction

      Lithium oxide is added to water.

      i. Balanced Equation

          ▸ $Li_2O + H_2O \rightarrow 2Li^+ + 2OH^-$

G. Hydrides of Group 1 and 2 with water

   1. Hydroxide with Hydrogen gas will be formed.
   2. pH will be basic.
   3. Exothermic reaction

      Potassium hydride is added to water.

      i. Balanced Equation

          ▸ $KH + H_2O \rightarrow K^+ + OH^- + H_2$

H. Precipitate double replacement reactions
   1. Question can have the terms "equimolar" and "precipitate."
   2. It is important to know solubility rules.
   3. Spectator ions are not included.
      A solution of sodium chloride and silver nitrate are mixed and a precipitate forms.
      i. Balanced Equation
          ▸ $Ag^+ + Cl^- \rightarrow AgCl$

I. Heating of a hydrate to form anhydride and water.
   1. Anhydride—compound formed by the removal of water.
      Cobalt (II) nitrate hexahydrate is heated.
      i. Balanced Equation
          ▸ $Co(NO_3)_2 \cdot 6H_2O \rightarrow Co(NO_3)_2 + 6H_2O$

J. Metals and an acid combine to produce hydrogen gas.
   1. Spectator ions are not included.
      i. Balanced Equation
          ▸ $Mg + 2H^+ \rightarrow Mg^{2+} + H_2$
   Magnesium is reacted with dilute hydrochloric acid.

K. Metals and water produce the metallic hydroxide and hydrogen gas.
   1. Spectator ions are not included.
      i. Balanced Equation
          ▸ $Ca + 2H_2O \rightarrow Ca^{2+} + 2OH^- + H_2$
   Solid Calcium is added to water, producing heat.

L. Hydrolysis of metal sulfide by water
   1. Hydroxide is produced, increasing pH of solution.
   Potassium sulfide hydrolyzes in water.
      i. Balanced Equation
          ▸ $K_2S + 2H_2O \rightarrow H_2S + 2K^+ + 2OH^-$

III. Flame Test Colors

1. To help solve questions that include data regarding elements.

Ion	Color
Li	Red
Na	Yellow
K	Violet/Purple
Ca	Orange
Sr	Red
Ba	Green
Cu^{2+}	Blue-Green
Fe	Gold
P	Blue-Green

One of the biggest obstacles you will have to overcome on the AP Chemistry exam is problem No. 4 in the free-response section. In addition to writing the balanced chemical equation, a follow-up question, worth 1 point, will be asked about each reaction. This question could be a short calculation or a laboratory observation.

Relationships in the Periodic Table

I. Relationships in the Periodic Table

A. Periodicity

1. Periodicity—classifying the chemical properties of elements that occur at regular intervals.

Sample AP Questions

Questions 1–3 refer to the following orbitals in gaseous atoms in the ground state.

(A) 1s

(B) 2p

(C) 3d

(D) 4s

(E) 5f

1. The element occupying valence electrons in this orbital have a formula of $X(OH)_2$

2. Identifies a radioactive element

3. Elements with electrons in this orbital form various colors based on oxidation states

Questions 4–5 refer to the following:

    (A) Transition Elements

    (B) Halogens

    (C) Noble Gases

    (D) Alkali Metals

    (E) Alkaline Earth Metals

4. Have very low energy associated with them

5. Otherwise known as salt formers

6. The elements Boron and Gallium have similar properties because of which of the following?

    (A) They are in the same group and have the similar molar masses.

    (B) They are in the same group and have the same number of valence electrons.

    (C) They are in the same period and have the same number of valence electrons.

    (D) They are both metals.

    (E) There is no relationship between the elements that can be deduced from the periodic table.

7. The electronegativity values of 4 different elements are shown below. Which of the following is the closest to being non-polar?

Elements	Electronegativity
N	3.0
H	1.0
I	2.7
S	2.5

(A) N–H

(B) H–I

(C) H–S

(D) N–S

(E) N–I

Questions 8–10 refer to atoms with the ground state electron configurations shown below.

(A) $1s^2 2s^2 2p^6 3s^1$

(B) $1s^2 2s^2 2p^4$

(C) $1s^2 2s^2 2p^6 3s^2 3p^6 4s^2 3d^{10} 4p^6 5s^2 4d^{10} 5p^6$

(D) $1s^2 2s^2 2p^6 3s^2 3p^6 4s^2 3d^{10} 4p^5$

(E) $1s^2 2s^2 2p^6 3s^2 3p^6 3d^{10} 4p^6 5s^2 4f^4$

8. Can re-ignite a glowing splint

9. Halogen

10. Xe

11. In the periodic table, the trend in the atomic radius from Magnesium to Phosphorus is which of the following?

   I.   Increases from Magnesium to Phosphorus

   II.   Decreases from Magnesium to Phosphorus

   III. Increases from Phosphorus to Magnesium

   IV.   Decreases from Phosphorus to Magnesium

   V.   Stays the same

(A) I only

(B) II only

(C) II and III

(D) I and IV

(E) V

Questions 12–15 refer to the following elements at 25°C and 1 atm.

(A)   Sulfur

(B)   Mercury

(C)   Phosphorus

(D)   Chlorine

(E)   Potassium

12. Rapid oxidation when exposed to air

13. Powerful oxidant used as disinfectant

14. Liquid metal at STP

15. Yellow crystalline solid that can be used in fertilizers

16. Which elements have nearly the same atomic radius?

(A)   Li, Be, O

(B)   Be, Mg, Ca

(C) N^{3-}, F^-, Ne

(D) Al^{3+}, Mg^{1+}, Ne

(E)   K, Ca, Ga

Test Tip

Periodicity requires knowing the trends from Chapter 2 along with a few facts about some important elements. Don't be surprised if these questions end up in the multiple-choice section of the exam.

Answers to Sample AP Questions

1. (D) Element would be Ca forming $Ca(OH)_2$
2. (E) Actinides
3. (C) Transition elements
4. (C) Noble gases have filled orbitals.
5. (B) NaCl, KI are examples of salt formers.
6. (B) All elements in the same group have chemical reactivity based on valence electrons.
7. (E) 0.3 for N–I
8. (B) Oxygen
9. (D) 7 valence electrons
10. (C) Full octet of electrons
11. (C) Trend is left to right decrease, or right to left increase
12. (E) Alkali Metal property
13. (D) Chlorine is found in bleach.
14. (B) Property of Hg
15. (A) Sulfates
16. (C) All have the same number of valence electrons, therefore all have the same atomic radius.

Organic Chemistry

I. Introduction to Organic Chemistry

A. Hydrocarbons

1. Compounds made of hydrogen and carbon.
2. Range from solids, to liquids, to gases.
3. All hydrocarbons are non water-soluble.
4. All hydrocarbons are flammable.

B. Alkanes

1. Types of hydrocarbons that have a general formula of C_nH_{2n+2}.
2. Colorless molecules
3. Non-polar
4. Alkanes increase in melting and boiling point with molecular weight.
5. Involved in combustion reactions releasing CO_2 and H_2O.

Name	Molecular Formula	Structural Formula
Methane	CH_4	CH_4
Ethane	C_2H_6	CH_3-CH_3
Propane	C_3H_8	CH_3-CH_2-CH_3
Butane	C_4H_{10}	CH_3-CH_2-CH_2-CH_3
Pentane	C_5H_{12}	CH_3-CH_2-CH_2-CH_2-CH_3
Hexane	C_6H_{14}	CH_3-CH_2-CH_2-CH_2-CH_2-CH_3
Heptane	C_7H_{16}	CH_3-CH_2-CH_2-CH_2-CH_2-CH_2-CH_3
Octane	C_8H_{18}	CH_3-CH_2-CH_2-CH_2-CH_2-CH_2-CH_2-CH_3
Nonane	C_9H_{20}	CH_3-CH_2-CH_2-CH_2-CH_2-CH_2-CH_2-CH_2-CH_3
Decane	$C_{10}H_{22}$	CH_3-CH_2-CH_2-CH_2-CH_2-CH_2-CH_2-CH_2-CH_2-CH_3

C.   Structural Isomers

1. Molecules that have the same chemical formula, but a different structural formula.

2. All alkanes, starting with propane, can be drawn different ways, and, therefore, have structural isomers.

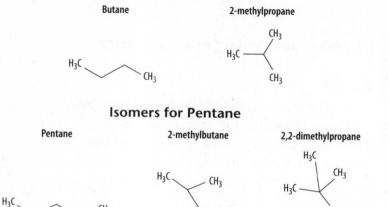

Isomers for Butane

Butane   2-methylpropane

Isomers for Pentane

Pentane   2-methylbutane   2,2-dimethylpropane

D. Optical isomers—Mirror images of a molecule that cannot be superimposed onto each other. Carbon atom is attached to *four different groups*. This is called an *asymmetric carbon atom* or sometimes a *chiral carbon atom*.

Optical Isomer of alanine

E. Cycloalkanes

1. Tetrahedral carbons formed into a ring
2. General formula is C_nH_{2n}.

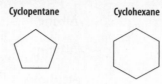

Cyclopentane   Cyclohexane

F. Alkenes

1. Hydrocarbons that have a C = C double bond
2. General formula is C_nH_{2n}
3. Display geometric isomerism based on C = C double bond

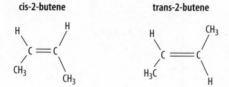

cis-2-butene   trans-2-butene

G. Alkynes

1. Hydrocarbons that have a C ≡ C triple bond
2. A general formula is C_nH_{2n-2}

Ethyne   Propyne

HC ≡ CH   HC ≡ C — CH₃

H. Benzene

1. Aromatic compound with unpleasant odor
2. One of the top chemicals produced in the United States.
3. Precursor for many types of compounds

Benzene

I. Functional groups

Functional Group	Name of Compound	Representative Structure
C=C	Alkene	$H_2C = CH_2$
C≡C	Alkyne	$HC \equiv CH$
C—OH	Alcohol	$H_3C — OH$
C—N	Amine	$H_3C — NH_2$
$\overset{\overset{O}{\|\|}}{C — H}$	Aldehyde	$H_3C — \overset{\overset{O}{\|\|}}{C} — H$
$\overset{\overset{O}{\|\|}}{C — C — C}$	Ketone	$H_3C — \overset{\overset{O}{\|\|}}{C} — CH_3$
$\overset{\overset{O}{\|\|}}{C — OH}$	Carboxylic Acid	$H_3C — C \overset{O}{\underset{OH}{}}$
$\overset{\overset{O}{\|\|}}{C — O — C}$	Ester	$H_3C — \overset{\overset{O}{\|\|}}{C} — O — CH_3$
$\overset{\overset{O}{\|\|}}{C — N}$	Amide	$H_3C — \overset{\overset{O}{\|\|}}{C} — NH_2$

Test Tip

Some AP teachers will spend too much time reviewing organic chemistry because they enjoyed their organic chemistry class in college. Beware of this! Know what is in this chapter and move on.

PART VI:

LABORATORY AND CHEMICAL CALCULATIONS

Making Observations

I. Studying Chemical Reactions

A. Observations that lead to evidence of a chemical reaction

1. Disappearance of reactant, or appearance of product.
2. Heat is produced (exothermic) or consumed (endothermic).
3. Color change.

B. Predicting Chemical Reactions

1. Solubility Rules—rules that indicate which atoms or ions are soluble in water and thus can participate in a chemical reaction.
2. There are several rules that you must memorize in order to accurately write and/or predict chemical reactions.

Positive Ion (cation)	Negative Ions (anion)	Soluble in Water?	Example
Alkali Metals (Li^+, Na^+, K^+, Rb^+, Cs^+)	All anions	Yes	NaCl, LiOH
H^+ ion	All anions	Yes	HCl, H_3PO_4
NH_4^+ (ammonium)	All anions	Yes	NH_4OH
Any cation	Nitrate-NO_3^-	Yes	$Mg(NO_3)_2$

Continued →

(Continued from previous page)

Positive Ion (cation)	Negative Ions (anion)	Soluble in Water?	Example
Any cation	Acetate-$C_2H_3O_2^-$	Yes, but $AgC_2H_3O_2$ moderately soluble	$NaC_2H_3O_2$
Ag^+, Hg_2^{2+}, Pb^{2+}, Cu^+	Cl^-, Br^-, I^-	Insoluble	–
Ag^+, Ca^{2+}, Sr^{2+}, Ba^{2+}, Hg_2^{2+}, or Pb^{2+}	Sulfate-SO_4^{2-}	Insoluble	–
Any cation	Perchlorate-ClO_4^-	Soluble	$Al(ClO_4)_3$
Any cation	Chlorates-ClO_3^-	Soluble	$NaClO_3$

▸ All phosphates (PO_4^{3-}) are insoluble except those containing alkali metals or ammonium.
▸ All carbonates (CO_3^{2-}) are insoluble except those containing alkali metals or ammonium.
▸ Hydroxides (OH^-) with alkali metals are soluble, but those containing Ca^{2+}, Sr^{2+}, or Ba^{2+} are moderately soluble.
▸ All chromates (CrO_4^{2-}) are insoluble except those containing alkali metals or ammonium.
▸ All sulfides (S^{2-}) are insoluble except those containing alkali metals, alkaline earth metals, and ammonium.
▸ All sulfites (SO_3^{2-}) are insoluble except those containing alkali metals or ammonium.

C. Synthesis Reactions

   1. A + B → AB
   2. Two or more substances combine to form a new compound.
      i. Metal + Nonmetal → Binary Ionic Compound
         $Mg\ (s) + Cl_2(g) \rightarrow MgCl_2(s)$

ii. Nonmetal + Nonmetal → Covalent Bonds
$$H_2(g) + F_2(g) \rightarrow 2HF(l)$$

D. Decomposition Reactions

1. AB → A + B
2. A compound breaks down into two or more substances.
3. Thermal decomposition is the most common type found on the AP test.
    i. Decomposition by electricity into elements.
        ‣ $2NaCl(s) \rightarrow 2Na(s) + Cl_2(g)$
    ii. Oxy-acids, when heated, decompose to form water and the nonmetal oxide.
        ‣ $H_2CO_3(aq) \rightarrow H_2O(l) + CO_2(g)$
    iii. Metallic chlorates, when heated, decompose to form metal chloride and oxygen gas.
        ‣ $2KClO_3(s) \rightarrow 2KCl(s) + 3O_2(g)$
    iv. Metallic hydroxides, when heated, decompose to form the metal oxide and water.
        ‣ $Ca(OH)_2(aq) \rightarrow CaO(s) + H_2O(l)$
    v. Metallic carbonates, when heated, decompose to form the metal oxide and carbon dioxide
        ‣ $Li_2CO_3(aq) \rightarrow Li_2O(s) + CO_2(g)$
    vi. Metallic oxides are stable, but a few decompose when heated to form the metal and oxygen gas.
        ‣ $2HgO(s) \rightarrow 2Hg(l) + O_2(g)$

E. Single Replacement Reactions

1. A + BX → AX + B
2. Elements replace elements in a compound.
    i. More reactive metal replacing another metal in solution
        ‣ $2Li(s) + MgCl_2(aq) \rightarrow 2LiCl(aq) + Mg(s)$
    ii. Metal with acid to produce hydrogen gas.
        ‣ $2Na(s) + 2HCl(aq) \rightarrow 2NaCl(aq) + H_2(g)$
    iii. Halogen replacing halogen (more reactive $F_2 > Cl_2 > Br_2 > I_2$ less reactive)
        ‣ $F_2(g) + 2KI(aq) \rightarrow I_2(s) + 2KF(aq)$

F. Double Replacement Reactions

1. AB + CD → AD + CB
2. Happens when 2 ionic compounds are mixed together.
3. The anions of one compound react with the cations of the other compound.
4. Products of double replacement reactions can be a precipitate (solid), water or a gas.
   i. Classic Example
      ‣ $2KI(aq) + Pb(NO_3)_2(aq) → 2KNO_3(aq) + PbI_2(s)$
   ii. Acid-Base Neutralization Reaction
      ‣ $HCl\ (aq) + NaOH(aq) → H_2O\ (l) + NaCl(aq)$

G. Combustion Reaction

1. Hydrocarbon + Oxygen → Water and Carbon Dioxide
2. Also called burning.
   i. Example of burning ethane
      ‣ $2C_2H_6(g) + 7O_2(g) → 4CO_2(g) + 6H_2O(g)$

H. Problem 4 of the Free-Response Section of the Exam

1. You will be required to write the balanced chemical equations for 3 reactions.
2. You must assume all solutions are aqueous.
3. Represent all solutions as ions in your answer.
4. Omit ions or formulas that are unchanged.

Test Tip

There will be one question on balancing chemical equations in the multiple-choice section, and problem 4 of the free-response section will be a reaction question. You should be prepared, though, to have to classify reactions into one of the several types explained and predict the products of a chemical reaction from words. Do not forget about the precipitation reactions and redox reactions explained in earlier chapters.

Recording Data

I. Significant Figures

A. AP directions indicate that in all free-response questions requiring a calculation, significant figures should be paid attention to.

B. Digits that are significant

1. All non-zero digits are significant.
   Example: 200 has one significant digit, while 891.2 has four significant digits.
2. Zeros between non-zero digits are significant.
   Example: 150.101 has six significant figures.
3. Leading zeros are not significant.
   Example: 0.00091 has two significant figures: 9 and 1
4. Trailing or end zeros in a number containing a decimal point are significant.
   Example: 3.1500 has five significant figures: 3, 1, 5, 0 and 0.
   Example: 0.000623900 still has only six significant figures (the zeros before the 6 are not significant).
   Example: 314.00 has five significant figures, making it clear that two decimals of accuracy were intended.
5. A decimal point after a number indicates significant figures.
   Example: 100. indicates three significant figures.

C. Significant figures in calculations

1. Addition and Subtraction
   i. Based on the least number of digits after the decimal point.

    ii.   The uncertainty is based on the least precise measurement. In other words, you cannot be more precise than your least precise measurement.

        Examples:

          (1) 45.67 g + 2.1356 g + 14.1 g = 61.9056 g = 61.9 g reported to the correct number of significant figures.

          (2) 12 ft + 56.34 ft + 23.4 ft = 91.74 ft = 92 ft reported to the correct number of significant figures.

2. Multiplication and Division

    i.   Based on the number with the smallest amount of significant figures.

        Examples:

          (1) 43.2 m $\times$ 34.567 m = 1493.2944 m = 1.49 $\times$ 10^3 m^2 reported to the correct number of significant figures (powers of ten are not significant).

          (2) 34.1 g divided by 2.1 L = 16 g/L reported to the correct number of significant figures.

3. Exact Numbers

    i.   Defined numbers that have no bearing in determining significant figures. For example, 12 in = 1 ft is an exact number and not measured.

4. Precision

    i.   Refers to repeatability.

    ii. Refers to the ability to show the same result each time.

    iii. Precision does *not* necessarily mean you are accurate.

5. Accuracy

    i.   The degree of closeness to achieving the measured or known value.

    ii. If you are accurate, by default, you must have been precise.

Laboratory Example of Accuracy and Precision

A known piece of copper with a mass of 3.67g was measured by three separate groups of students three times. The example below shows various accounts of accuracy and precision.

Low Precision Low Accuracy	High Precision Low Accuracy	High Precision High Accuracy
4.56 g	2.50 g	3.65 g
1.34 g	2.47 g	3.70 g
2.22 g	2.51 g	3.68 g

6. Percent Difference Formula—a measurement of precision

   i. $\text{Percent Difference} = \dfrac{(\text{Large Value} - \text{Small Value})}{\text{Average Value}} \times 100$

7. Percent Error Formula—a measurement of accuracy

   i. $\text{Percent error} = \dfrac{(\text{Experimental Value} - \text{Known Value})}{\text{Known Value}} \times 100$

Test Tip

Any good chemistry student should have found this chapter relatively easy to assimilate. The AP readers will reward you if you accurately record data by using significant figures, accuracy, and precision in your answers to free-response questions.

Calculations

I. Percent Difference Calculation

Two different chemistry students were measuring the mass of a substance in two similar 100 mL beakers. This was accomplished using an analytical balance and the following data was recorded.

Student 1—24.543 g

Student 2—23.108 g

▶ Determine the percent difference between the two.

▶ The Percent Difference Formula is a measurement of precision (between two measurements).

▶ $Percent\ Difference = \dfrac{(Large\ Value - Small\ Value)}{Average\ Value} \times 100$

▶ $Percent\ Difference = \dfrac{(24.543\ g - 23.108\ g)}{23.826\ g} \times 100 = 6.023\%$

II. Percent Error Calculation

The known mass of a 100 mL beaker is 23.986 g. Based on the data above, which student is more accurate? Explain with a calculation.

▶ The Percent Error Formula is a measurement of accuracy.

▶ $Percent\ error = \dfrac{(Experimental\ Value - Known\ Value)}{Known\ Value} \times 100$

▶ Student 1:

$$Percent\ error = \frac{(24.583\ g - 23.986\ g)}{23.986\ g} \times 100 = 2.4890\%$$

▶ Student 2:

$$Percent\ error = \frac{(23.108\ g - 23.986\ g)}{23.986\ g} \times 100 = 3.6605\%$$

Student 1 is more accurate.

These formulas will not be given to you in the reference portion of the AP Chemistry exam, so it's best for you to memorize them.

Communication of Results

I. Communication of Results

A. In various multiple-choice questions and free-response questions, an analysis of tabular data may have to be done in order to answer a question correctly.

B. Since you have performed laboratory experiments in your class, follow a sequential sequence to fill in the table if need be.

C. If the data is already contained within the table, you will most likely use it for a calculation of graphical analysis.

Example: The data below reflects the results of heating a metal oxide to drive off oxygen from the sample. Assume that no oxygen is remaining in the sample after heating. Answer the questions below.

Line		Trial #1
1	Mass of crucible and lid, g	16.721 g
2	Mass of crucible, lid, and metal oxide, g	31.786 g
3	Mass of metal oxide , g	Subtract Line 1 from Line 2 = 15.065 g
4	Mass of crucible, lid, and metal, g (after heating)	25.760 g

↑
This column is placed for readability purposes. IT WILL NOT BE ON THE TEST.

Continued →

(Continued from previous page)

Line		Trial #1
5	Mass of metal produced, g	Subtract Line 1 from Line 4 = 9.039 g
6	Mass of oxygen produced, g	Subtract Line 5 from Line 3 = 6.026 g

(1) According to the table above, determine the following:
    i.   The mass percent of oxygen in the metal oxide.
    ii. Of the metals listed below, which is most likely to be found in the metal oxide?

$$\frac{6.026 \; g \; oxygen}{15.065 \; g \; metal \; oxide} \times 100 = 40.00\%$$

    (A)   Na (MM = 23 g/mol)

    (B)   K (MM = 39 g/mol)

    (C)   Ca (MM = 40 g/mol)

    (D)   Mg (MM = 24 g/mol)

    (E)   Li (MM = 7 g/mol)

Since 40% by mass is oxygen the metal must be 60% of the sample. A quick molar mass calculation indicates that MgO (60% Mg and 40% O) is the metal oxide. The correct answer is (D).

D. Density and significant figures using tabular data

Example: A known mass of Ni metal was dropped into a graduated cylinder that is filled with water. Using the portion of the graduated cylinder marked in milliliters below, along with the table, answer the following questions.

	Trial #1
Mass of metal, g	40.086 g
Volume of water before addition of metal, g	Part A
Volume of water after addition of metal, g	Part B

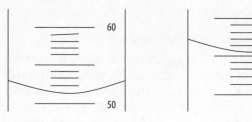

Before addition of solid   After addition of solid

(1) Determine the volume of water before the addition of the Ni metal (Part A)?

▸ Read meniscus: 51.0 mL

Determine the volume of water after the addition of the Ni metal (Part B)?

▸ Read meniscus: 55.5 mL

Determine the density of the metal to the correct number of significant figures.

▸ *Volume of Ni metal = 4.5 mL*

▸ *Density of metal =* $\dfrac{mass}{volume} = \dfrac{40.086\ g}{4.5\ mL} = 8.9\ \dfrac{g}{mL}$

E. Dimensional Analysis or Factor-Label

1. A systematic mathematical method used to organize your calculations in a logical manner.

2. Using correct dimensional analysis is key for earning maximum points on the free-response section of the test.

3. Method is helpful for stoichiometric calculations as well as basic unit conversions.

4. Dimensional analysis is the best method to communicate your calculations on the test. Use it!!!

Example: Convert 0.72 g of N to atoms of N

$$\frac{0.72\ \cancel{g\ N}}{1} \times \frac{1\ \cancel{mole\ N}}{14\ \cancel{g\ N}} \times \frac{6.022 \times 10^{23}\ atoms}{1\ \cancel{mole\ N}} = 3.1 \times 10^{22}\ atoms$$

F. Lab Equipment

1. Common lab equipment will be referenced on the test.
2. You may not be asked specifically about the function of each piece of equipment, but this sort of thing will most likely be used in questions. Having a good working knowledge of basic chemistry equipment will give you an advantage.

Name of Equipment	Picture	Function
Beaker		Glass used to hold and heat solutions. Not used for measuring.
Buchner Funnel		Used for suction filtration along with a filtering flask.
Bunsen Burner		Produces a flame for heating.
Burette		Used for volumetric delivery of solutions. Used in titration experiment. Stopcock is small handle that controls the delivery of liquid.

Name of Equipment	Picture	Function
Clamp and Ring Stand		Holds funnels, flasks, wire gauze for burning.
Crucible		Heat resistant container used to heat compounds. Can be used in combination with ring stand and clamp.
Distillation Apparatus		Used to separate a mixture of compounds based on boiling point.
Erlenmeyer Flask		Conical piece of lab equipment that is used for holding liquids. Not used for measuring.

Continued →

(Continued from previous page)

Name of Equipment	Picture	Function
Filtering Flask		Used in combination with vacuum suction and Buchner funnel.
Funnel		Along with filter paper can be used to separate solids from liquids.
Hot Plate		Electric device that allows for controlled delivery of heat. Often contains a metallic stirrer to allow for mixing.
Mortar and Pestle		Porcelain piece of equipment that can be used for crushing and grinding.

Name of Equipment	Picture	Function
Separatory Funnel		Allows for the separation of immiscible liquids.
Thermometer		Used to read temperature.
Volumetric Flask		Used to accurately prepare solutions of various concentrations.

There is a high probability that a multi-part calculation free-response question will be asked on the test. There could be up to 7 parts on this question, with 3 to 5 of them requiring a calculation. Be systematic when answering this question and look for tabular data to help you answer the question correctly.

Percent Composition

I. Percent Composition

A. Definition—the composition by mass of each element in a compound relative to the total mass of the compound.

B. Example Problem 1—Straightforward

    i. Determine the percent composition of each element in $MgBr_2$ (atomic masses Mg = 24.3, Br = 79.9).

      ▸ *Molar Mass of $MgBr_2$ = 184.1 g/mol*

      ▸ $1 \; mol \; Mg = \dfrac{24.3 \, g}{184.1 \, g} \times 100 = 13.2\%$

      ▸ $2 \; mol \; Br = \dfrac{159.8 \, g}{184.1 \, g} \times 100 = 86.8\%$

C. Example Problem 2—Straightforward

    i. What is the percent of Al in aluminum oxide? (atomic masses Al = 27, O = 16).

      ▸ *Molar Mass of Al_2O_3 = 102 g/mol*

      ▸ $2 \; mol \; Al = \dfrac{54 \, g}{102 \, g} \times 100 = 53\%$

D. Example Problem 3—Complicated

    i. A 1.00g pure sample of limestone is dissolved in an acidic solution. If 0.43g of carbon dioxide is generated and no other carbonate is present, what is the percent of $CaCO_3$ by mass?

      ▸ Must write the chemical equation

$$CaCO_3(s) + 2H^+(ag) \xrightarrow{\text{Acid}} CO_2(g) + H_2O(l) + Ca^{+2}(aq)$$

$$\frac{0.43\ g\ CO_2}{1} \times \frac{1\ mol\ CO_2}{44\ g\ CO_2} \times \frac{1\ mol\ CaCO_3}{1\ mol\ CO_2} \times \frac{100\ g\ CaCO_3}{1\ mol\ CaCO_3} \times 100 = 98\%$$

E. Example Problem 4—Moderate

    i.   A certain drug is 71.0% C, 14.0% H, and 16.0% N. What mass of each element can be recovered from a 25.0 g sample of the drug?

               $0.710 \times 25.0\ g = 17.8\ g\ C$

               $0.140 \times 25.0\ g = 3.5\ g\ H$

               $0.160 \times 25.0\ g = 4.00\ g\ N$

Test Tip

Percent composition is a standard question on the AP Chemistry exam. This concept is easily worth 2 questions on the AP test. Use your knowledge of percents and solve the questions correctly.

Empirical and Molecular Formula

I. Empirical and Molecular Formula

A. Empirical Formula—the simplest expression of the relative numbers of each type of atom in a compound. The simplest whole number ratio of atoms of each element present in a compound.

B. Molecular Formula—a multiple of the empirical formula based on the actual number of atoms of each type in the compound. For example, if the empirical formula of a compound is CH_2, its molecular formula may be C_2H_4, C_5H_{10}.

C. Example Problem 1—Straightforward

1. A compound was analyzed and found to contain 30% N and 70% O by mass. What is the empirical formula?

$$30\% \, N = \frac{30 \, g \, N}{1} \times \frac{1 \, mol \, N}{14 \, g \, N} = 2.14 \, mol \, N$$

$$70\% \, O = \frac{70 \, g \, O}{1} \times \frac{1 \, mol \, O}{16 \, g \, O} = 4.38 \, mol \, O$$

$$\frac{2.14 \, mol \, N}{2.14} = 1, \quad \frac{4.38 \, mol \, O}{2.14} = 2$$

$Formula = NO_2$

D. Example Problem 2—Moderate

1. A 5.271g sample of a compound was found to contain 2.477g of N and 2.793g of O. The molecular mass of the compound is 210 g/mol. Determine the molecular formula.

$$\frac{2.477\,g\,N}{1} \times \frac{1\,mol\,N}{14\,g\,N} = 0.1769\,mol\,N$$

$$\frac{2.793\,g\,O}{1} \times \frac{1\,mol\,O}{16\,g\,O} = 0.1746\,mol\,O$$

$$\frac{0.1769\,mol\,N}{0.1746} = 1, \quad \frac{0.1746\,mol\,O}{0.1746} = 1$$

$$\textit{Empirical Formula} = NO = 30\frac{g}{mol}$$

$$\textit{Molecular Formula} = \frac{210}{30} = 7$$

$$7 \times NO + N_7O_7$$

E. Example Problem 3—Gas Laws

1. A hydrocarbon gas with empirical formula CH_2 has a density of 3.75 g/L at 0°C and 1 atm. Find the molecular formula of the hydrocarbon.

$$\frac{3.75\,g}{L} \times \frac{22.4\,L}{1\,mol} = 84.0\frac{g}{mol}$$

$$CH_2 = 14.0\frac{g}{mol}$$

$$\frac{84\frac{g}{mol}}{14\frac{g}{mol}} = 6$$

$$6 \times CH_2 = C_6H_{12}$$

F. Example Problem 4—Straightforward

1. A compound contains 0.90 mol Li, 0.45 mol Se, and 1.35 mol S. What is the simplest formula of the compound?

$$\frac{0.90\,mol\,Li}{0.45} = 2, \quad \frac{0.45\,mol\,Se}{0.45} = 1, \quad \frac{1.35\,mol\,S}{0.45} = 3$$

$$\textit{Formula} = Li_2SeS_3$$

G. Example Problem 5—Straightforward

1. Vitamin C consists of C, H, and O in the following percentages: 41.0%, 4.50%, and 54.5%. If the molar mass of Vitamin C is 176 g/mol, determine the molecular formula of Vitamin C.

$$\frac{41.0\,g\,C}{12} = 3.42\,mol\,C, \frac{4.5\,g\,H}{1} = 4.5\,mol\,H, \frac{54.5\,g\,O}{16} = 3.41\,mol\,O$$

$$\frac{3.42\,mol\,C}{3.41} = 1\,mol\,C, \frac{4.5\,mol\,H}{3.41} = 1.32\,mol\,H, \frac{3.41\,mol\,O}{3.41} = 1\,mol\,O$$

Multiply by 3 to make whole number ratio of $C_3H_4O_3 = 88\frac{g}{mol}$

$$\frac{176\frac{g}{mol}}{88\frac{g}{mol}} = 2 \times C_3H_4O_3 = C_6H_8O_6$$

H. Example Problem 6—Complicated

1. Methyl acrylate or Plexiglass is a commonly used product as an impact-resistant form of glass. In a one gram sample of Plexiglass, there is 0.56 g C, 0.07 g H, and 0.37 g O. If 0.312g of Plexiglass is contained in 0.0036 mol, determine the molecular formula of Plexiglass.

$$\frac{0.56\,g\,C}{12} = 0.047\,mol\,C, \frac{0.07\,g\,H}{1} = 0.07\,mol\,H, \frac{0.37\,g\,O}{16} = 0.023\,mol\,O$$

$$\frac{0.047\,mol\,C}{0.023} = 2\,mol\,C, \frac{0.07\,mol\,H}{0.023} = 3\,mol\,H, \frac{0.023\,mol\,O}{0.023} = 1\,mol\,O$$

Empirical Formula $= C_2H_3O = 43\frac{g}{mol}$

Molecular Formula Molar Mass $= \frac{0.312\,g}{0.0036\,mol} = 87\frac{g}{mol}$

$$\frac{87\frac{g}{mol}}{43\frac{g}{mol}} = 2 \times C_2H_3O = C_4H_6O_2$$

Test Tip

Practice and understand the examples above and you have covered a major calculation that is on the AP Chemistry Exam.

Molar Masses

I. Molar Mass

A. Molar Mass is key to several AP Chemistry problems both directly and indirectly.

B. Molar Mass = grams of substance/one mole of substance.

C. Gas Law Questions with Molar Mass

1. See Chapter 7, Gas Law

D. Molar Mass of Hydrates

1. When $CoCl_2 \cdot xH_2O$ is heated, 45.4% of its mass is lost. What is the formula of the hydrate?

   If 45.4% of mass is lost, then that mass has to be evaporated water. The percent mass of $CoCl_2$ must be 54.6%.

   x = molar mass of compound

   $x(.546) = 130$ g/mol (molar mass of $CoCl_2$), $x = 238.1$ g/mol

   238.1 g/mol $- 130$ g/mol $= 108.1$ g of water

   $$\frac{108.1\,g\,water}{18\frac{g}{mol}} = 6\,mol\,H_2O$$

2. When 0.125 moles of $CaSO_4 \cdot xH_2O$ is heated, 4.5 g of water is lost, what is the value of x or the number of moles of water?

   $$0.125\ moles = \frac{1}{8}\ of\ a\ mole$$

   $8 \times 4.5\ g = 36 = 2\ mole\ H_2O$

E. Find the Molar Mass of an Element Using the Law of Definite Composition

1. When the mass of element X is found in 1 mole of 4 different compounds the following amounts are found: 36 grams, 54 grams, 72 grams, and 90 grams.

   What is the molar mass (atomic weight) of element X?

   (A) 12

   (B) 18

   (C) 24

   (D) 36

   (E) 54

   Need to find a molar mass that will produce a whole number coefficient of moles for each mass. The correct answer is (B).

F. Molarity

1. What is the mass of Li_2SO_4 (110 g/mol) required to prepare 30mL of 0.20M $LiSO_4$?

$$Molarity = \frac{Mole}{Liter}$$

$$\frac{0.0300\,L}{1} \times \frac{0.2\,mol\,Li_2So_4}{1\,L\,Li_2So_4} \times \frac{110\,g\,Li_2So_4}{1\,mol\,Li_2So_4} = 0.66\,g\,Li_2So_4$$

G. Using Boiling Point Elevation and Molality to Find Molar Mass

1. A solution is prepared by adding 1.24 grams of substance X in 100g of benzene. The solution has a boiling point of 80.45°C. Benzene has a normal boiling point of 80.1°C. Determine the molar mass of substance X.

$$Elevation\ of\ boiling\ point = \Delta t_{bp} = K_{bp} \cdot m_{solute}$$

$$K_{bp} = molal\ boiling\ point\ constant$$

$$m_{solute} = molality\ of\ solute$$

$$\Delta t_{bp} = 80.45°C - 80.1°C = 0.35°C$$

$$K_{bp} \text{ benzene} = 2.53 \frac{°C}{m}$$

$$0.35°C = 2.53 \frac{°C}{m} \cdot m_{solute}$$

$$m_{solute} = 0.14 \ m$$

$$\frac{0.14 \text{ mol solute}}{1 \text{ kg solvent}} \times 0.100 \text{ kg benzene} = 0.014 \text{ mole solute}$$

$$\frac{1.24 \ g}{0.014 \text{ mole}} = 88.6 \frac{g}{mol} \text{ (substance X)}$$

H. Using Freezing Point Depression and Molality to Find Molar Mass

   1. In order to lower the freezing point of water by 10.0°C, 1500 g of substance M is added to 6.00 kg of water. Find the molar mass of substance M.

$$\text{Depressing of freezing point} = \Delta t_{fp} = K_{fp} \cdot m_{solute} \cdot i$$

K_{fp} = molal freezing point constant

m_{solute} = molality of solute

i = van't Hoff factor

$$\Delta t_{fp} = 0.00°C - 10.0°C = -10.0°C$$

$$K_{fp} \text{ water} = -1.86 \frac{°C}{m}$$

$$-10.0°C = -1.86 \frac{°C}{m} \cdot m_{solute}$$

$$m_{solute} = 5.4m$$

$$\frac{5.4 \text{ mole solute}}{1 \text{ kg solvent}} \times 6.00 \text{ kg water} = 32 \text{ mole solute}$$

$$\frac{1500 \ g}{32 \text{ moles}} = 47 \frac{g}{mol} \text{ (substance M)}$$

Test Tip

Molar mass is easy to remember. However, on the AP Chemistry test, you must anticipate being asked to calculate molar mass through several methods or use it to solve for another important chemistry concept.

Gas Law Calculations

I. Gas Law Calculations

A. Of the 6 free-response questions on the AP Chemistry exam, the historical pattern is that Gas Law Calculations are going to be asked in conjunction with other AP chemistry topics.

B. Sample AP Question—Gases #1

When magnesium metal is added to hydrochloric acid, a gas and salt are produced. Assume that an AP Chemistry student added 34.56 g of magnesium metal to excess hydrochloric acid. Answer the following:

    i.   Write a balanced chemical equation for the reaction.

$$Mg(s) + 2HCl(aq) \rightarrow MgCl_2(aq) + H_2(g)$$

        Net Ionic equation:

$$Mg(s) + 2H^+(aq) \rightarrow Mg^{2+}(aq) + H_2(g)$$

    ii.   Calculate the number of grams of gas that are produced.

$$\frac{34.56\ g\ Mg}{1} \times \frac{1\ mol\ Mg}{24.3\ g\ Mg} \times \frac{1\ mol\ H_2}{1\ mol\ Mg} \times \frac{2.0\ g\ H_2}{1\ mol\ H_2} = 2.844\ g\ H_2$$

    iii.   What volume would the gas occupy if collected at 30°C and 92.7 kPa?

$$PV = nRT$$

$$(0.92\ atm)(V) = (1.42\ mol\ H_2)\left(0.0821\ \frac{L \cdot atm}{mol \cdot K}\right)(303\ K)$$

$$V = 38.4\ L$$

C. Sample AP Question—Gases #2

A 20.4 g sample of a gas with empirical formula C_2H_4Cl is placed in a 2.00L gas vessel at 2.00 atm and 30°C. Determine the molecular formula of the gas.

$$PV = nRT$$

$$(2.00\ atm)(2.00\ L) = (n)\left(0.0821\ \frac{L \cdot atm}{mol \cdot K}\right)(303\ K)$$

$n = 0.161\ mol$

C_2H_4Cl molar mass = 63.5 g/mol

$$Unknown\ Gas\ molar\ mass = \frac{20.4\ g}{0.161\ mol} = 127\ g/mol$$

$$\frac{127}{63.5} = 2$$

$Formula = 2 \times C_2H_4Cl = C_4H_8Cl_2$

D. Sample AP Question—Gases #3

Answer the questions below based on the following balanced chemical equation.

$$SiO_2(s) + 2H_2O(g) \rightarrow SiH_4(g) + 2O_2(s)$$

i. The above reaction takes place at 30°C and 0.5 atm in a 2.1 L container. How many grams of H_2O will react with SiO_2?

$$PV = nRT$$

$$(0.50\ atm)(2.1\ L) = (n)\left(0.0821\ \frac{L \cdot atm}{mol \cdot K}\right)(303\ K)$$

$n = 0.042\ mol\ SiO_2$

$$\frac{0.042\ mol\ SiO_2}{1} \times \frac{2\ mol\ H_2O}{1\ mol\ SiO_2} \times \frac{18\ g\ H_2O}{1\ mol\ H_2O} = 1.5\ g\ H_2O$$

ii. Determine the partial pressure of both product gases assuming the reaction goes to completion.

Using stoichiometry 0.042 mole SiO_2 will produce the following:

$$\frac{0.042 \; mol \; SiO_2}{1} \times \frac{1 \; mol \; SiH_4}{1 \; mol \; SiO_2} = 0.042 \; mol \; SiH_4$$

$$\frac{0.042 \; mol \; SiO_2}{1} \times \frac{2 \; mol \; O_2}{1 \; mol \; SiO_2} = 0.084 \; mol \; O_2$$

Total moles = 0.126

$$P_{SiH_4} = \frac{0.042 \; mol \; SiH_4}{0.126 \; mol} (0.5 \; atm) = 0.17 \; atm$$

$$PO_2 = 0.50 \; atm - 0.17 \; atm = 0.33 \; atm$$

Stoichiometric Calculations

I. Stoichiometric Calculations

A. Of the 6 free-response questions on the AP Chemistry exam, the historical pattern is that stoichiometry will be asked in conjunction with other AP Chemistry topics.

B. Sample AP Question—Stoichiometry #1

Answer the following questions that relate to the burning of acetylene gas, C_2H_2, in a gas vessel.

$$2\ C_2H_2(g) + 5\ O_2(g) \rightarrow 2\ H_2O(g) + 4\ CO_2(g)$$

(A) A 21.1 L sample of C_2H_2 (g) at 2.00 atm and 100°C is combined with 150 g O_2.

   (i) How many moles of C_2H_2 are available to react?

$$PV = nRT$$

$$(2.00\ atm)(21.1\ L) = n\left(0.0821\ \frac{L \cdot atm}{mol \cdot K}\right)(373\ K)$$

$$n = 1.38\ mole\ C_2H_2$$

   (ii) What is the limiting reactant for the reaction? Use calculations.

$$\frac{1.38\ mol\ C_2H_2}{1} \times \frac{2\ mol\ H_2O}{2\ mol\ C_2H_2} = 1.38\ mol\ H_2O$$

$$\frac{150\ g\ O_2}{1} \times \frac{1\ mol\ O_2}{32\ g\ O_2} \times \frac{2\ mol\ H_2O}{5\ mol\ O_2} = 1.88\ mol\ H_2O$$

Limiting Reagent is C_2H_2

   (iii) How many moles of water are formed?

$$1.38\ mol\ H_2O$$

(iv) In a reaction vessel, 0.200 M $MgSO_4$ and 0.300 M H_3PO_4 are combined to a final volume of 3L with water.

$$3\ MgSO_4(aq) + 2\ H_3PO_4(aq) \rightarrow Mg_3(PO_4)_2(s) + 3H_2SO_4(aq)$$

(v) Calculate the mass of $Mg_3(PO_4)_2$ formed?

$$\frac{3\ L}{1} \times \frac{0.200\ mol\ MgSO_4}{1\ L\ MgSO_4} \times \frac{1\ mol\ Mg_3(PO_4)_2}{3\ mol\ MgSO_4} \times \frac{263\ g\ Mg_3(PO_4)_2}{1\ mol\ Mg_3(PO_4)_2}$$

$$= 52.6\ g\ Mg_3(PO_4)_2$$

$$\frac{3\ L}{1} \times \frac{0.300\ mol\ H_3PO_4}{1\ L\ H_3PO_4} \times \frac{1\ mol\ Mg_3(PO_4)_2}{2\ mol\ H_3PO_4} \times \frac{263\ g\ Mg_3(PO_4)_2}{1\ mol\ Mg_3(PO_4)_2}$$

$$= 118\ g\ Mg_3(PO_4)_2$$

Only 52.6 g mol $Mg_3(PO_4)_2$ can be produced since $MgSO_4$ is the limiting reagent.

(vi) Calculate the pH of the reaction, assuming it goes to completion. Use calculations.

Since $MgSO_4$ is the limiting reagent, this can be used to find the molarity of H_2SO_4.

$$\frac{3\ L}{1} \times \frac{0.200\ mol\ MgSO_4}{1\ L\ MgSO_4} \times \frac{3\ mol\ H_2SO_4}{3\ mol\ MgSO_4} = 0.600\ mol\ H_2SO_4$$

$$\frac{0.600\ mol\ H_2SO_4}{3\ L} = 0.200\ M\ H_2SO_4$$

H_2SO_4 is a strong acid that completely disassociates, so the concentration of $H^+ = (.2M)(2) = 0.400\ M$.

$pH = -log[H^+] = -log\ 0.400 = 0.397$

(vii) What is the concentration of the sulfate ion, assuming the reaction goes to completion?

The concentration of the sulfate ion remains unchanged from the beginning of the reaction.

$$0.200\ M\ H_2SO_4 = 0.200\ M\ SO_4^{2-}$$

C. Sample AP Question—Stoichiometry #2

Answer the following questions that relate to the synthesis for carbon monoxide from elemental carbon.

$$2C(s) + O_2(g) \rightarrow 2\ CO(g) + 188\ kCal$$

(A) If 4.1×10^{23} atoms of C react with excess oxygen, producing noxious carbon monoxide, determine the following:

(i) How many molecules of CO will be produced?

$$\frac{4.1 \times 10^{23} \text{ atoms } C}{1} \times \frac{1 \text{ mol } C}{6.022 \times 10^{23} \text{ atoms } C} \times \frac{2 \text{ mol } CO}{2 \text{ mol } C} \times \frac{6.022 \times 10^{23} \text{ molecules } CO}{1 \text{ mol } CO}$$

$$= 4.1 \times 10^{23} \text{ molecules } CO$$

(ii) What volume of O_2 gas will react with C at STP?

$$\frac{4.1 \times 10^{23} \text{ atoms } C}{1} \times \frac{1 \text{ mol } C}{6.022 \times 10^{23} \text{ atoms } C} \times \frac{1 \text{ mol } O_2}{2 \text{ mol } C} \times \frac{22.4 \text{ L } O_2}{1 \text{ mol } O_2}$$

$$= 7.6 \text{ L } O_2$$

(iii) How much heat is generated in this reaction based on 4.1×10^{23} atoms of C?

$$\frac{4.1 \times 10^{23} \text{ atoms } C}{1} \times \frac{1 \text{ mol } C}{6.022 \times 10^{23} \text{ atoms } C} \times \frac{188 \text{ kCal}}{2 \text{ mol } C} = 64.0 \text{ kCal}$$

(iv) Draw the Lewis Structure of CO.

10 total valence electrons

$$:C \equiv O:$$

(v) If excess heat is added to the reaction, predict the direction of the reaction and describe why.

Le Chatelier's principle states that a change in one of the variables that describe a system at equilibrium produces a shift in the position of the equilibrium that counteracts the effect of this change. Since the reaction is exothermic, adding heat can be counteracted by shifting the reaction toward the reactant. An exothermic reaction mimics adding excess product to the system.

Test Tip

Stoichiometry on the free-response section of the AP exam requires the use of a calculator, thus you'll find these problems in Part A of the free-response section. Be leery of concepts such as pH, Lewis Structure, equilibrium, and gases, which will be additional components of the problem.

Mole Fraction/Partial Pressure Calculations

I. **Mole Fraction/Partial Pressure Calculations**

A. Of the six free-response questions, the historical pattern is that Mole Fraction/Partial Pressure Calculations will be asked in conjunction with other AP Chemistry topics.

B. Sample AP Question—Mole Fraction/Partial Pressure #1

A rigid 7.00 L container contains 32.45 g CO_2 gas and 15.5 g O_2 gas.

  i. Calculate the total pressure in atmospheres of the gas mixture at 10°C.

$$32.45 \, g \, CO_2 = 0.74 \, mol \, CO_2$$
$$15.5 \, g \, O_2 = 0.48 \, mol \, O_2$$
Total moles = 1.22

$$PV = nRT$$

$$(P)\,(7.00 \; L) = (1.22 \, mol)\left(0.0821 \, \frac{L \cdot atm}{mol \cdot K}\right)(283 \, K)$$

$$P = 4.05 \, atm$$

  ii. Assume the temperature of the mixture stays the same. Calculate the following.

    a. The mole fraction of each gas in the sample.

$$\frac{0.74 \, mol \, CO_2}{1.22 \, mol} = 0.61$$

$$\frac{0.48 \, mol \, O_2}{1.22 \, mol} = 0.39$$

b. The partial pressure of each gas in the sample.
PP of CO_2 = 0.61 (4.05 atm) = 2.47 atm
PP of O_2 = 0.39 (4.05 atm) = 1.58 atm

C. Sample AP Question—Mole Fraction/Partial Pressure #2

Two flasks are shown below connected by a stopcock. The 4.0L flask contains NO_2 and the 2.0L flask contains O_2. The respective pressures are listed below. Calculate the total pressure of the system after the stopcock is opened.

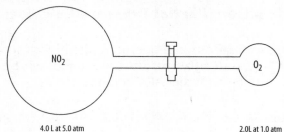

4.0 L at 5.0 atm   2.0L at 1.0 atm

$$Pressure\ of\ NO_2 = \frac{(5.0\ atm)(4.0\ L)}{6.0\ L} = 3.3\ atm$$

$$Pressure\ of\ O_2 = \frac{(1.0\ atm)(2.0\ L)}{6.0\ L} = .33\ atm$$

Total pressure = 3.3 atm + 0.33 atm = 3.6 atm

D. Sample AP Question—Mole Fraction/Partial Pressure #3

Nitrogen monoxide is thermally decomposed into its gaseous elements. Answer the following questions.

1. Write a balanced equation for this reaction.

$$2NO(g) \rightarrow N_2(g) + O_2(g)$$

2. 456 mL of the products of this reaction are collected over water at 21.0°C and 3.4 atm. Find the partial pressure of each dry gas.

(Dalton's Law of Partial Pressure)

$$3.4\ atm = P_{N_2} + P_{O_2} + P_{H_2O}$$

At 21.0°C vapor pressure of water = 0.025 atm

$$3.4 \ atm = P_{N_2} + P_{O_2} + 0.025 \ atm$$

$$P_{N_2} + P_{O_2} = 3.38 \ atm$$

The mole ratio of N_2 to O_2 is 1 to 1, so each contributes 1.69 atm of pressure.

Test Tip

In each released AP Chemistry exam, a partial pressure/mole fraction has been either a multiple-choice or a free-response question. Therefore, this is a salient concept that you should not ignore when studying for the exam.

Faraday's Laws

I. Faraday's Law

A. *Electromotive Force (emf)*—electrons that are created at the anode (site of oxidation) flow toward the cathode through this force.

B. Electrons move from a high potential energy (anode) to a low potential energy (cathode).

C. Moving electrons provide work given by the formula:
   Electrical Work = charge $\times$ potential energy difference

D. Charge is measured in coulombs (C) and one electron is 1.6022×10^{-19} C in charge.

E. *Volt*—one joule of work is performed when one coulomb passes through a potential difference of one volt.

II. Relationship Between E° and ΔG°

A. $\Delta G°_{rxn} = -nFE°$

   n = number of moles transferred between oxidizing and reducing agents

   F = Faraday's constant = 9.6485×10^4 J/V · mol

Sample AP Problem

The reaction of zinc metal and copper (II) ions has an $E°$ of 1.10V at standard temperature. Calculate the ΔG for the reaction.

$$Zn(s) + Cu^{2+}(aq) \rightarrow Zn^{2+} + Cu(s)$$

$$\Delta G°_{rxn} = -nFE°$$

$$\Delta G°_{rxn} = -(2 \text{ mol electrons})\left(\frac{9.65 \times 10^4 J}{V \cdot mol}\right)(1.10 V)\left(\frac{1 \text{ } kJ}{1000 \text{ } J}\right)$$

$$= -212 \text{ } kJ$$

Test Tip

The relationship between $E°$ and $\Delta G°$ has been on two of the last four released AP Chemistry tests. The information can be found in the thermochemistry portion of your textbook and in the thermochemistry portion of the AP reference sheet.

Equilibrium

I. Equilibrium Calculations

A. Question No. 1 on the free-response section is guaranteed to be based on chemical equilibrium. This section allows you to use your calculator and frequently has various other AP topics mixed with the equilibrium question.

B. Sample AP Question—Equilibrium #1

A pure 1.72 g sample of a weak acid of HNO_2 (nitrous acid) is dissolved in enough water to make 250 mL of solution.

  i. Calculate the molar concentration of HNO_2.

$$\frac{1.72\,g\,HNO_2}{1} \times \frac{1\,mol\,HNO_2}{47\,g\,HNO_2} = \frac{0.0366\,mol\,HNO_2}{0.250\,L} = 0.146\,M\,HNO_2$$

Aqueous nitrous acid reacts with water according to the equation below:

$$HNO_2(aq) + H_2O(l) \leftrightarrow H_3O^+(aq) + NO_2^-(aq)$$
$$K_a = 6.0 \times 10^{-4}$$

  ii. Write the equilibrium-constant expression for the reaction of $HNO_2(aq)$ and water.

$$K_a = \frac{[NO_2^-][H_3O^+]}{HNO_2}$$

 iii. Determine the pH of the solution in part i.

Equation	HNO_2	H_3O^+	NO_2^-
Initial moles	0.146	0	0
Change	−x	+x	+x
Equilibrium moles	0.146-x	+x	+x

$$K_a = \frac{[x][x]}{0.146-x} = 6.0\times10^{-4}$$

Assume $x < 0.146$

$x^2 = (6.0 \times 10^{-4})(0.146)$

$x = 0.0094 = H_3O^+$

$pH = -\log[H_3O^+] = -\log 0.0094 = 2.03$

DO NOT USE QUADRATIC FORMULA

C. Sample AP Question—Equilibrium #2

$HA(aq)+H_2O(l) \leftrightarrow H_3O^+(aq) + A^- (aq)$ $K_a = 7.2 \times 10^{-4}$

A weak monoprotic acid, HA(aq), dissociates in water as represented above.

  i.   Write the equilibrium constant-expression for the dissociation of HA(aq) in water.

$$K_a = \frac{[A^-][H_3O^+]}{HA}$$

  ii.   Calculate the molar concentration of H_3O^+ in 0.25M HA(aq) solution.

$$K_a = \frac{[x][x]}{0.25} = 7.2\times10^{-4}$$

$x^2 = 1.8 \times 10^{-4}$

$x = 0.013 = H_3O^+$

  iii.   Calculate the pH of the solution.

$$pH = -\log[H_3O^+] = -\log 0.013 = 1.89$$

The test makers may substitute the following equilibrium constant expressions in question 1: K_c, K_p, K_a, K_b, K_{sp}. Historical data indicates that you will have to set up the expression, solve for a concentration or pressure, and then use other AP concepts to maximize your score. This question may force you to look for equations on the reference sheet. If you don't have a copy of the reference sheet that will accompany the exam, go to the AP Chemistry exam description on the College Board website and download it. Be sure to familiarize yourself with the information before your exam.

Nernst Equation

I. Nernst Equation

A. Standard Potential/E°—the measure of the overall potential difference or voltage with all substances at 1.0M concentration.

B. The Nernst Equation is used as a correction factor for aqueous substances that are NOT at 1.0M concentration. Non-standard potential is called E_{nst}.

   i.   Nernst Equation

$$E_{nst} = E^0 - \frac{RT}{nF} \ln Q = E^0 - \frac{0.0592}{n} \log Q$$

$$Q = reaction\ quotient = \frac{[C]^c [D]^d}{[A]^a [B]^b}, \quad aA + bB \rightarrow cC + dD$$

where
   $R = ideal\ gas\ law\ constant$
   $T = temperature\ in\ Kelvin$
   $n = number\ of\ electrons\ transferred$
   $F = Faradays\ constant = 96\ 500\ columbs\ per$
   $\qquad mole\ of\ electrons$

Sample AP Question

Calculate E_{nst} for the following:

2Ag⁺(aq, 0.60M) + Hg(l) → Ag(s) +Hg²⁺(aq, 0.0015M)

Reduction: 2Ag⁺(aq) + 2e⁻ → 2Ag(s) $E^0 = 0.800V$

Oxidation: Hg(l) → Hg²⁺+ 2e⁻ $E^0 = -0.855V$ (switch sign)

2Ag⁺(aq) + Hg(l) → Hg²⁺(aq) + 2Ag(s) $E^0 = -0.055V$

$$E_{nst} = -0.055V - \frac{0.0592}{2} \log \frac{(0.0015)^1}{(0.60)^2} = 0.015V$$

Product favored since the sign for E_{nst} is positive

Test Tip

The Nernst Equation looks difficult, but it's all about plug and chug. Plug in the given formula, which will be on the reference sheet, and let your calculator do the rest.

Thermochemistry

I. Thermochemistry Calculations

A. Of the 6 free-response questions, the historical pattern is that thermochemistry is going to be asked in conjunction with other AP Chemistry topics.

B. Sample AP Question—Thermochemistry #1

$$NH_4Cl(s) \leftrightarrow NH_3(g) + HCl(g)$$
$$\Delta H_{298} = 176 \text{ kJ/mol}; \Delta G_{298} = 91.2 \text{ kJ/mol}$$

The following questions relate to the balanced chemical equation in the box above.

(a) Calculate the standard entropy change for the reaction.

$$\Delta G^\circ_{298} = \Delta H^\circ_{298} - T\Delta S^\circ_{298}$$

$$91.2 \frac{kJ}{mol} = 176 \frac{kJ}{mol} - 298(\Delta S^0_{298})$$

$$\Delta S^\circ_{298} = 0.285 \frac{kJ}{mol}$$

(b) Calculate the standard enthalpy change that occurs when 4.20 mol sample of $NH_4Cl(s)$ is decomposed at 298K.

$$\frac{4.20 \text{ mol } NH_4Cl}{1} \times \frac{176 \text{ kJ}}{1 \text{ mol } NH_4Cl} = 739 \frac{kJ}{mol}$$

(c) Using the grid below, complete the potential energy diagram for the reaction above. Indicate the ΔH for the reaction.

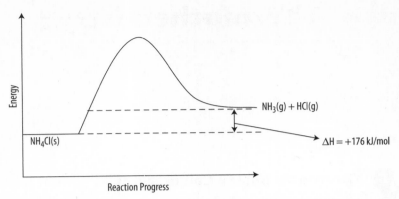

(d) Assuming the mixture is at equilibrium, what would be the effect of increasing the temperature of the mixture?

Le Chatelier's principle states that a system will counteract a stressor. If heat is "added" to the system (initially endothermic), the result would favor the formation of the products or the endothermic reaction.

C. Sample AP Question—Thermochemistry #2

In order to determine the specific heat of a certain metal, a chemist uses a block of ice along with a 45.6 g piece of metal. The metal is heated from 0°C to 90°C and placed on the block of ice. After the metal cools back to 0°C, 6.74 g of ice is melted. Determine the specific heat of the metal. The heat of fusion for ice is 334 J/g.

Use heat of fusion:

$$\frac{334 \, J}{g} \times 6.74 \, g = 2250 \, J$$

Use $q = m(\Delta T)c_p$

$$2250J = (45.6 \, g)(90°)c_p$$

$$c_p = 0.549 \, \frac{J}{g \, °C}$$

Thermochemistry is a vast topic and highly likely to be on the AP Chemistry exam. By studying this chapter and reviewing Chapter 15, "Thermodynamics," you'll be able to "burn" through these questions.

Kinetics

I. Kinetic Calculations

A. The historical pattern of the free-response questions shows that kinetics is going to be asked in conjunction with other AP Chemistry topics.

B. Sample AP Question—Kinetics #1

Answer the following questions related to the kinetics of chemical reactions.

$$A(aq) + B(aq) \rightarrow C(aq) + D(aq)$$

Trial	[A] mol/L	[B] mol/L	Rate of the formation of C in mol/L/s
1	0.023	0.020	0.00213
2	0.071	0.020	0.00639
3	0.022	0.078	0.00852

(a) Determine order for the following reactants

i.   A

$$\frac{rate\ trial\ 2}{rate\ trial\ 1} = \frac{k[A]^x\ trial\ 2}{k[A]^x\ trial\ 1}$$

$$\frac{0.00639}{0.00213} = \frac{k\,[0.071]^x\ trial\ 2}{k\,[0.023]^x\ trial\ 1}$$

$$3 = \frac{[0.071]^x\ trial\ 2}{[0.023]^x\ trial\ 1} = 3.09^x,\ therefore\ x = 1$$

1st order for A

ii.

B

$$\frac{rate\ trial\ 3}{rate\ trial\ 1} = \frac{k[B]^x\ trial\ 3}{k[B]^x\ trial\ 1}$$

$$\frac{0.00852}{0.00213} = \frac{k\,[0.078]^x\ trial\ 3}{k\,[0.020]^x\ trial\ 1}$$

$$4 = \frac{[0.078]^x\ trial\ 3}{[0.020]^x\ trial\ 1} = 4^x, \text{ therefore } x = 1$$

1st order for B

(b) For the reaction

i. Write the rate law based on trial 1 and calculate the rate constant.

$$Rate = k[A][B]$$
$$0.00213 = k(0.023)(0.020)$$
$$k = 4.6$$

ii. Sketch a graph depicting the order of the reaction.

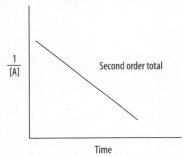

Second order total

$\frac{1}{[A]}$

Time

Test Tip

Kinetics questions can appear as multiple-choice questions or free-response questions. For either type of question, be sure to follow the steps as described in Chapter 14.

Chapter 4

Major AP Chemistry Laboratory Themes and Their Relationship to the Test

(Each of the labs described below fulfills the objectives of the College Board-recommended experiments.)

Lab 1: Determination of the Formula of Compound

Synopsis of Experiment: Students will drive off the oxygen in a sample of silver oxide using a crucible and Bunsen burner. When silver oxide is heated, silver will be left in the crucible with oxygen escaping into the atmosphere. A simple table is constructed to keep track of the massed samples.

	Trial #1
Mass of crucible and lid, g	25.217
Mass of crucible, lid, and silver oxide, g	27.418
Mass of silver oxide, g	2.201
Mass of crucible, lid, and silver metal, g (after heating)	27.264
Mass of silver produced, g	2.047
Mass of oxygen produced, g	0.154
Moles of silver produced	0.01897
Moles of oxygen produced	0.009625
Mole ratio of silver to oxygen	1.97:1
Empirical Formula	Ag_2O

Calculations

Trial 1

$$\frac{2.047 \ g \ Ag}{1} \times \frac{1 \ mol \ Ag}{107.9 \ g \ Ag} = 0.01897 \ mol \ Ag$$

$$\frac{0.154 \ g \ O}{1} \times \frac{1 \ mol \ O}{16.0 \ g \ O} = 0.009625 \ mol \ O$$

Mole Ratio

$$\frac{0.01897 \ mol \ Ag}{0.009625} = 1.97 \ mol \ Ag$$

$$\frac{0.009625 \ mol \ O}{0.009625} = 1 \ mol \ O$$

The empirical formula for silver oxide is Ag_2O.

▸ The balanced chemical equation for the thermal decomposition of silver oxide is below:

$2Ag_2O(s) \rightarrow 4Ag(s) + O_2(g)$

Lab 2: Determination of the Percentage of Water in a Hydrate

Synopsis of Experiment: Students will drive off the water in a sample of alum using a crucible and Bunsen burner. When alum (hydrate) is heated, the anhydrate $AlK(SO_4)_2$ will be left in the crucible, with water escaping into the atmosphere. A simple table is constructed to keep track of the massed samples.

	Trial #1
Mass of crucible and lid, g	22.879
Mass of crucible, lid, and alum, g	24.879
Mass of alum, g	2.000
Mass of crucible, lid, and $AlK(SO_4)_2$, g (after heating)	23.959

	Trial #1
Mass of $AlK(SO_4)_2$ produced, g	1.080
Mass of water produced, g	0.920
Moles of $AlK(SO_4)_2$ produced	0.004181
Moles of water produced	0.0511
Mole ratio of $AlK(SO_4)_2$ to water	1:12.2

Calculations

Trial 1

$$\frac{1.080\ g\ AlK(SO_4)_2}{1} \times \frac{1\ mol\ g\ AlK(SO_4)_2}{258.3\ g\ AlK(SO_4)_2} = 0.004181\ mol\ g\ AlK(SO_4)_2$$

$$\frac{0.920\ g\ H_2O}{1} \times \frac{1\ mol\ g}{18.0\ g\ H_2O} = 0.0511\ mol\ H_2O$$

Mole Ratio

$$\frac{0.004181\ mol\ g\ AlK(SO_4)_2}{0.004181} = 1\ mol\ AlK(SO_4)_2$$

$$\frac{0.0511\ mol\ H_2O}{0.004181} = 12.2\ mol\ H_2O$$

The empirical formula for Alum is $AlK(SO_4)_2 \cdot 12H_2O$.

▸ In $AlK(SO_4)_2 \cdot 12H_2O$ 54% by mass is $AlK(SO_4)_2$ and 46% by mass is H_2O.

Lab 3: Determination of the Molar Mass of Volatile Liquids

Synopsis of Experiment: A small amount of the volatile liquid (acetone MM = 58 g/mol) is placed in a plastic pipet and allowed to vaporize using boiling water. Condensed liquid vapor is then collected by allowing the pipet to cool and the sample is massed. The volume of the pipet is calculated using the density of water and the mass of the sample of water placed in the pipet. A rearrangement of the Ideal Gas Law Equation allows for the calculation of the molar mass of the volatile liquid. A simple table is constructed to keep track of the massed samples.

Boiling Water Bath Temperature = 100.0°C = 373K

Barometric Pressure = 750 mm Hg = 0.99 atm

Room Temperature = 22.0°C = 295K

Density of Water = 0.9971 g/mL

Mass of empty pipet,g	1.768
Mass of pipet and water,g	17.983
Mass of water,g	16.215
Volume of pipet*	Volume = 16.26 mL = 0.01626 L

$$0.9971 \frac{g}{mL} = \frac{16.215\,g}{v}, \text{ Volume} = 16.26 \text{ mL} = 0.01626 \text{ L}$$

Acetone	Trial 1
Mass of empty pipet,g	1.768
Mass of pipet and condensed acetone,g	1.799
Mass of acetone,g	0.0312
Molar Mass of acetone,g/mol	59.4

$PV = nRT$

$$n = \frac{mass}{molar\ mass}$$

$$molar\ mass\left(\frac{g}{mol}\right) = \frac{mass \times RT}{P \times V}$$

$$*D = \frac{m}{v}$$

Trial 1

$$molar\ mass\left(\frac{g}{mol}\right)=\frac{0.031\,g\times0.0821\dfrac{L\cdot atm}{mol\cdot K}\times373K}{(0.99\,atm)\,(0.01626\,L)}=60\,g\,/\,mol$$

Lab 4: Molar Mass by Freezing Point Depression

Synopsis of Experiment: Colligative properties of solutions are based on the number of dissolved particles rather than the type of particle. Freezing point, or the temperature that changes a state of matter from liquid to solid, is a colligative property that can be used to calculate the molar mass of a substance. Freezing point change is directly proportional to the molality (m) of a substance.

Molality is defined as moles of solute divided by the kilograms of solvent:

Equation 1: $m=\dfrac{moles(solute)}{kg(solvent)}$

Moles of the solute are equal to grams divided by molar mass and can be substituted into the equation above:

Equation 2: $m=\dfrac{g(solute)}{kg(solvent)\times molar\ mass(solute)}$

The change in freezing point is defined as:

Equation 3: $\Delta T_{fp}=k_{fp}\times m$

(k_{fp} = *freezing point depression constant, m = molality*)

Combining equations 2 and 3 gives you the following:

$$Molar\ Mass\ (solute)=\frac{k_{fp}\times g(solute)}{kg(solvent)\times\Delta T_{fp}}$$

Sample Calculation

Solvent: para-dichlorobenzene

Freezing Point of pure solvent: 53.0°C

Mass of unknown substance: 1.75 g

Freezing point depression constant: $7.1°C/m$

Mass of para-dichlorobenzene: 23.23 g

Freezing point of solution: 50.1°C

$$\Delta T_{fp} = 53.0°C - 50.1°C = 2.9°C$$

$$Molar\ Mass\ (solute) = \frac{k_{fp} \times g(solute)}{kg(solvent) \times \Delta T_{fp}}$$

$$Molar\ Mass\ (solute) = \frac{\left(7.1\frac{°C}{m}\right)(1.75\ g)}{(0.02323\ kg)\,(2.9°C)} = 184\ g/mol$$

Lab 5: Determination Molar Volume of a Gas

Synopsis of Experiment: Avogadro's Law states that equal volume of gases must contain equal numbers of molecules at the same temperature and pressure. The molar volume of any gas is known as 22.4 L of gas at STP. In this experiment, a sample of magnesium ribbon is placed in hydrochloric acid and the resulting gas is collected using a Gas Measuring Tube. Calculations are then made to determine the molar volume of hydrogen gas at STP.

Chemical Equation: $Mg(s) + 2HCl(aq) \rightarrow MgCl_2(aq) + H_2(g)$

Net Ionic Equation: $Mg(s) + 2H^+(aq) \rightarrow H_2(g) + Mg^{2+}(aq)$

	Trial 1	Trial 2
Mass of magnesium,g	0.053	0.048
Moles of magnesium	2.2×10^{-3}	2.0×10^{-3}
Moles of hydrogen produced*	2.2×10^{-3}	2.0×10^{-3}
Volume of H_2 gas produced	4.9×10^{-2}	4.3×10^{-2}
Molar volume of H_2 gas	22.4	21.7
Average Molar Volume	21.9	

*1 to 1 mole ratio in balanced chemical equation

Trial 1—Molar Volume Determination

$$\frac{4.9 \times 10^{-2} \, L \, H_2}{2.2 \times 10^{-3} \, mol \, H_2} = 22.3 \, mol / L$$

Trial 2—Molar Volume Determination

$$\frac{4.3 \times 10^{-2} \, L \, H_2}{2.0 \times 10^{-3} \, mol \, H_2} = 21.5 \, mol / L$$

$$Percent \, Error = \frac{(Experimental \, Value - Known \, Value)}{Known \, Value} \times 100$$

$$Percent \, Error = \frac{\left(21.9 \frac{L}{mol} - 22.4 \frac{L}{mol}\right)}{22.4 \frac{L}{mol}} \times 100 = -1.8\%$$

Labs 6 and 7: Acid-Base Titrations

Synopsis of Experiment: A titration is a standard laboratory technique used in chemistry to determine the concentration of an unknown solution. This experiment will require the student to "standardize" a known amount of NaOH and use that solution to titrate a known volume of HCl. The titrant in this experiment is NaOH and will be added drop by drop using a buret to HCl. As the NaOH is added, it is consumed by the HCl based on the neutralization reaction below.

$$NaOH(aq) + HCl(aq) \rightarrow NaCl(aq) + H_2O(l)$$

Once the exact stoichiometric amounts of NaOH are added to HCl, the equivalence point of the titration is reached. An indicator solution is added to the titration to detect the equivalence point. The endpoint of the titration is the point when the indicator changes color, which means that the equivalence point has been reached. In the reaction above, before NaOH is added, the solution has a pH that is less than 7. The pH changes to exactly 7 when the stoichiometric amount of NaOH is added. If too much NaOH is added, the pH of the solution will be greater than 7. The progress of the titration is measured via a titration curve that is plotted on a graph. When the acid is one-half neutralized, the pK_a of the acid can be calculated.

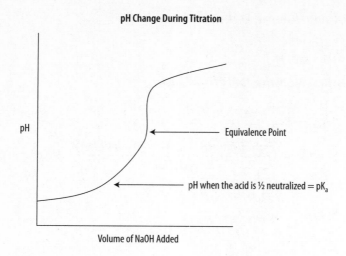

pH Change During Titration

pH

Equivalence Point

pH when the acid is ½ neutralized = pK$_a$

Volume of NaOH Added

Sample Titration Question:

Calculate the concentration of HCl if 32.0 mL of 1.5M NaOH is required to titrate 50.0 mL of the acid in order to reach the endpoint. The neutralization reaction is:

NaOH(aq) + HCl(aq) → NaCl(aq) + H$_2$O (l)

$$\frac{0.032\,L\,NaOH}{1} \times \frac{1.5\,mol\,NaOH}{1\,L\,NaOH} \times \frac{1\,mol\,HCl}{1\,mol\,NaOH} \times \frac{1}{0.050\,L\,HCl} = 0.96\,M\,HCl$$

Lab 8: Determination of Concentration by Oxidation-Reduction Titration

Synopsis of Experiment: In this experiment the student will determine the amount of substance present in a sample. The substance in the product can easily be oxidized using a strong oxidizing agent that will become reduced during the titration process. The oxidizing agent that will be used in this experiment is potassium permanganate or KMnO$_4$ and the manganese will be reduced from a +7 to a +2 oxidation state. The concentration of oxalic acid will be determined upon titration with KMnO4. The end point of the titration occurs when a pink color of MnO$_4^-$ persists in the solution.

Half Reactions

$$8H^+(aq) + MnO_4^-(aq) + 5e^- \rightarrow Mn^{2+}(aq) + 4H_2O(l) \text{ Reduction}$$
$$2H_2O(l) + H_2C_2O_4(aq) \rightarrow 2H_2CO_3(aq) + 2H^+(aq) + 2e^- \text{ Oxidation}$$

$$16H^+(aq) + 2MnO_4^-(aq) + 10e^- \rightarrow 2Mn^{2+}(aq) + 8H_2O(l) \text{ Reduction}$$
$$10H_2O(l) + 5H_2C_2O_4(aq) \rightarrow 10H_2CO_3(aq) + 10H^+(aq) + 10e^- \text{ Oxidation}$$

$$6H^+(aq) + 2MnO_4^-(aq) + 2H_2O(l) + 5H_2C_2O_4(aq) \rightarrow 2Mn^{2+}(aq) + 10H_2CO_3(aq)$$

	Trial 1
Volume of $H_2C_2O_4$ titrated, mL	25.00 mL
Initial volume of MnO_4^-, mL	0.60 mL
Final volume of MnO_4^-, mL	14.25 mL
Volume of MnO_4^- added, mL	13.65 mL

Molarity of MnO_4^- solution = 0.023

Determine the molarity of oxalic acid (OA) in trial 1.

$$\frac{0.01365\,L\,KMnO_4}{1} \times \frac{0.023\,mol\,KMnO_4}{1\,L\,KMnO_4} \times \frac{5\,mol\,OA}{2\,mol\,KMnO_4} \times \frac{1}{0.025\,L} = 0.031\,M\,OA$$

Lab 9: Determination of Mass and Mole Relationships in a Chemical Reaction

Synopsis of Experiment: In this experiment the concept of continuous variation is used to determine the mole ratios of two reactants in a chemical reaction. Three steps are involved in this experiment:

Step 1: Preparation of known concentration of reactants

Step 2: Mixing of reactants using different volume ratios

Step 3: The loss of reactant or gain of product is measured—gas formation, color change, precipitate.

The optimum ratio is found when the greatest amount of reactants is used and the most product is made. The reaction that will be used is between 0.5M solutions of $AgNO_3$ and K_2CrO_4. This reaction will produce a precipitate that can be dried and measured.

Trial	mL AgNO$_3$	mL K$_2$CrO$_4$	Grams Precipitate
1	2.5	23.0	1.1
2	7.5	17.5	2.3
3	12.5	12.5	4.7
4	15.0	10.0	6.2
5	17.5	7.5	5.0
6	20.0	5.0	3.5
7	23.0	2.5	1.7

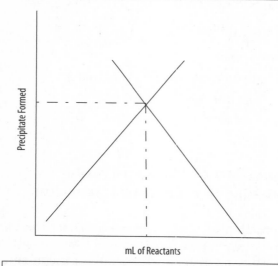

If the data is plotted on a graph, a line of best fit is created and the point(s) where the two lines intersect determines the coefficients for the reactants. If the data above is graphed, approximately 17 mL of AgNO$_3$ and 8.3 mL of K$_2$CrO$_4$ react, forming a 2:1 ratio.

The equation is

$$2AgNO_3(aq) + K_2CrO_4(aq) \rightarrow 2KNO_3(aq) + Ag_2CrO_4(s)$$

Lab 10: Determination of the Equilibrium Constant for a Chemical Reaction-K_a of Weak Acids

Synopsis of Experiment: Students will determine the K_a for a weak acid based on the ability of the acid to ionize hydrogen ions. The dissociation constant for the acid is a measure of the strength of the acid. A high K_a indicates a strong acid while a low K_a indicates a weak acid. The general formula and equilibrium expression for the ionization of an acid is below:

$$HA(aq) + H_2O(l) \rightleftarrows A^-(aq) + H_3O^+(aq)$$

$$K_a = \frac{[H_3O^+][A^-]}{[HA]}$$

Polyprotic acids such as H_2SO_4 and H_3PO_4 contain more than one ionizable hydrogen atom. When these acids ionize, the number of steps of ionization is based on the number of hydrogen atoms.

$$H_2A(aq) + H_2O(l) \rightleftarrows HA^-(aq) + H_3O^+(aq)$$

$$K_{a1} = \frac{[H_3O^+][HA^-]}{[H_2A]}$$

$$HA^-(aq) + H_2O(l) \rightleftarrows A^{2-}(aq) + H_3O^+(aq)$$

$$K_{a2} = \frac{[H_3O^+][A^{2-}]}{[HA^-]}$$

Students will add NaOH to one-half of a mixture of a weak acid and phenolphthalein solution until a pink color persists for 3–5 seconds. Once this takes place, the K_a of the solution can be determined because the beaker contains one-half the original amount of the acid (see previous experiment). The pH of the mixture is determined using a pH meter.

Weak Acid Name/Formula	K_a	pKa
Acetic Acid/$HC_2H_3O_2$	1.8×10^{-5}	4.74
Benzoic Acid/$HC_7H_5O_2$	6.5×10^{-5}	4.19
Glycolic Acid/$HC_2H_4O_2$	1.6×10^{-4}	3.80

Labs 11 and 19: Determination of the Appropriate Indicators for Various Acid-Base Titrations and Preparation and Properties of Buffer Solutions

Synopsis of Experiment (Lab 11): In the first experiment, students will determine the proper indicators to use for various titrations by conducting several different titration experiments with acids and bases.

Choice of Indicators

pH Indicator	Acid Color	Base Color	pH Transition Interval	Type of titration used for
Bromophenol Blue	Yellow	Blue	3.0–5.0	Strong Acid/ Weak Base Equivalence Point will be below 7.0
Bromothymol Blue	Yellow	Blue	6.0–7.6	Strong Acid/ Strong Base Equivalence Point will be exactly 7.0
Thymol Blue	Yellow	Blue	8.0–9.6	Weak Acid/ Strong Base Equivalence Point will be above 7.0
Phenolphthalein	Colorless	Red	8.0–10	Weak Acid/ Strong Base Equivalence Point will be above 7.0

Synopsis of Experiment (Lab 19): Solutions that contain a buffer resist changes in pH with the addition of an acid or base. Human blood has a crucial buffer system called the carbonic acid-hydrogen carbonate buffer system. This buffer system helps to maintain blood pH from 7.35 to 7.45. The carbonic acid-hydrogen carbonate buffer system is depicted below:

$$H^+(aq) + HCO_3^-(aq) \rightleftarrows H_2CO_3(aq) \rightleftarrows H_2O(l) + CO_2(g)$$

Lab 12: Determination of the Rate of the Reaction and its Order

Synopsis of Experiment: Students will determine how fast a chemical reaction will occur. The experiment is designed to study the kinetics involved in the oxidation of iodide ions by bromate ions in an acidic solution.

$$6I^-(aq) + BrO_3^-(aq) + 6H^+(aq) \rightarrow 3I_2(aq) + Br^-(aq) + 3H_2O(l)$$

The rate of this reaction depends on the temperature as well as the concentration of the reactants. To measure the rate of this particular reaction, students will measure the appearance of iodine as a product of the reaction. Starch reacts with iodine and produces a blue-black color that can be visually analyzed. Using time-based trials, the reaction rate, rate law, and activation energy will be determined.

▸ See Chapter 14 and Chapter 33 for examples of reaction rate calculations.

Lab 13: Determination of the Enthalpy Change Associated with a Reaction

Synopsis of Experiment: Students will determine the enthalpy change for a chemical reaction via Hess's Law. The enthalpy change is equal to the amount of heat transferred in a reaction. This enthalpy change can be calculated by the sum of the individual chemical reactions that make up the overall reaction. Since all reactions will occur in a solution, the following equations can be used to determine the enthalpy.

$$q = (mass)(c_p)(\Delta T)$$
$$q_{rxn} = -(q_{sol} + q_{cal})$$

The use of a coffee-cup calorimeter allows enthalpy change to be measured since it is a good insulator of released energy. Most of the heat released in chemical reactions will be absorbed by the solution, with a small amount being absorbed by the calorimeter.

Equation 1   ~~NaOH (aq)~~ + HCl(aq) → ~~NaCl(aq)~~ + ~~H₂O(l)~~

Equation 2   ~~H₂O(l)~~ +NH_3(aq) + ~~NaCl (aq)~~ → NH_4Cl (aq) + ~~NaOH (aq)~~

Equation 3 NH_3(aq) + HCl(aq) → NH_4Cl (aq)

▸ See Chapter 15 and Chapter 32 for examples of enthalpy change calculations.

Lab 14: Separation and Qualitative Analysis of Cations and Anions

Synopsis of Experiment: Students will determine the presence of certain cations and anions in a list of unknown solutions. Students are given 10 test tubes labeled 1-10 each containing a different sample of solution. All of the possible two test tube samples are placed together and analyzed for the evidence of a chemical reaction. Observations include: precipitate formation, heat evolved, gas production or no reaction.

Examples of Possible Results

Cations	Reagent	Result
Ag^+, Pb^{2+}, Hg_2^{2+}	6 M HCl	Precipitate will form
Cu^{2+}, Hg^{2+}, Sn^{2+}, Sn^{4+}	0.1 M H_2S pH 0.5	Precipitate will form
Ba^{2+} , Ca^{2+}, Mg^{2+}	0.2M $(NH_4)_2CO_3$, pH of 9.5	Precipitate will form

Labs 15 and 17: Synthesis of a Coordination Compound and Colorimetric or Spectrophotometric Analysis

Synopsis of Experiment: Students will prepare the coordination compound, tetraamminecopper(II) by reacting ammonia and copper(II) sulfate. The amount of pure tetraamminecopper(II) will be analyzed using a spectrophotometer. The maximum wavelength of absorbance will determine whether the correct compound has been formed.

Calculations:

1) The data and graph below indicate that the maximum absorbance spectrum for tetraamminecopper(II) is roughly 580nm, which is within the accepted value of 590 nm.

$$Percent\ Error = \frac{(Experimental\ Value - Known\ Value)}{Known\ Value} \times 100$$

$$Percent\ Error = \frac{(580 - 590)}{590} \times 100 = -1.7\%$$

Wave length (nm)	Absorbance
500	0.15
510	0.20
520	0.22
530	0.27
540	0.33
550	0.38
560	0.41
570	0.43
580	0.48
590	0.46
600	0.44
610	0.43
620	0.42
630	0.38

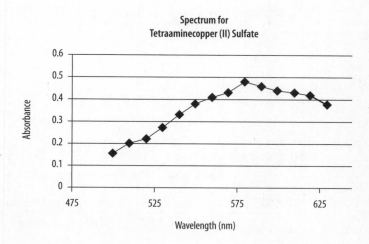

Spectrum for Tetraaminecopper (II) Sulfate

Lab 16: Analytical Gravimetric Analysis

Synopsis of Experiment: Students will separate silver metal from a Cu-Ag alloy using nitric acid as an oxidizing agent. The free silver will then be precipitated as silver chloride and filtered using a filter flask with a crucible attached. Gravimetric analysis is an important chemistry technique that allows the separation of a sample based on precipitation and filtering/washing techniques.

	Trial 1
Mass of alloy, g	0.4256
*Mass of NaCl needed to precipitate silver,g	0.2305
Mass of NaCl used,g	0.3457
Mass of dry filter and crucible,g	29.7560
Mass of crucible and AgCl,g	30.1560
Mass of AgCl,g	0.4000
Calculated mass of silver in silver chloride,g	75.24% by mass weight
**Calculated mass of silver in alloy,g	70.72% by mass weight

$$* \frac{0.4256 \ g \ Ag}{1} \times \frac{1 \ mol \ Ag}{107.9 \ g \ Ag} \times \frac{1 \ mol \ NaCl}{1 \ mol \ Ag} \times \frac{58.45 \ g \ NaCl}{1 \ mol \ NaCl} = 0.2305 \ g \ NaCl$$

$$** \frac{0.4000 \ g \ AgCl}{1} \times \frac{1 \ mol \ AgCl}{143.4 \ g \ AgCl} \times \frac{1 \ mol \ Ag}{1 \ mol \ AgCl} \times \frac{107.9 \ g \ Ag}{1 \ mol \ Ag} = 0.3010 \ g \ Ag$$

$$\frac{0.3010 \ g \ Ag}{0.4256 \ g \ AgCl} \times 100\% = 70.72\%$$

Lab 18: Separation by Chromatography

Synopsis of Experiment: Students separate mixtures of dyes based on differences in solubility. The components of the dyes will migrate differently on paper based on molecular interactions with the solute. The movement of the components of the dyes can be quantified using a formula called R_f or retention factor (R_f).

$$R_f = \frac{distance\ traveled\ by\ component\ (cm)}{distance\ traveled\ by\ solvent\ front\ (cm)}$$

Sample Results:

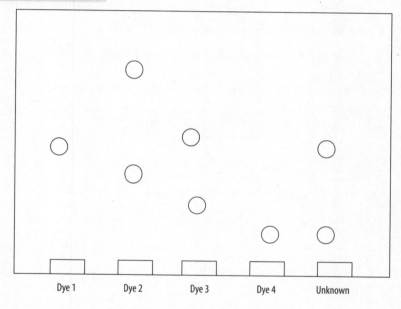

Dye 1   Dye 2   Dye 3   Dye 4   Unknown

Solvent front traveled 20 cm

Dye 1	Component 1 $R_f = 0.35$
Dye 2	Component 1 $R_f = 0.25$, Component 2 $R_f = 0.85$
Dye 3	Component 1 $R_f = 0.17$, Component 2 $R_f = 0.45$
Dye 4	Component 1 $R_f = 0.14$
Unknown	Mixture of dye 1 and 4 because it produces same results as those in dye 1 and 4

Labs 20 and 21: Determination of Electrochemical Series and Measurements Using Electrochemical Cells and Electroplating

Synopsis of Experiment: The transfer of electrons during a chemical reaction can be classified as an oxidation/reduction reaction. The loss of electrons indicates oxidation and the gain of electrons is classified as reduction (LEO the lion GERS). These labs can be summarized into 3 components.

1. Determining which elements produce a spontaneous redox reaction.

2. Creating an electrochemical cell.

3. Measuring potential difference across the cells.

Several different combinations of metals are listed below.

Anode	Cathode
Zn	Ag
Zn	Cu
Mg	Ag
Fe	Cu
Pb	Cu

Lab 22: Synthesis, Isolation, and Purification of an Organic Compound

Synopsis of Experiment: Students will react an organic acid with alcohol to produce an ester and water. The acid will be acetic acid and the alcohol will be methyl alcohol, producing methyl acetate. Stoichiometric calculations are made after maximum absorbance is calculated at a particular wavelength. Beer's Law is then used to calculate the concentration of the product at a given absorbance.

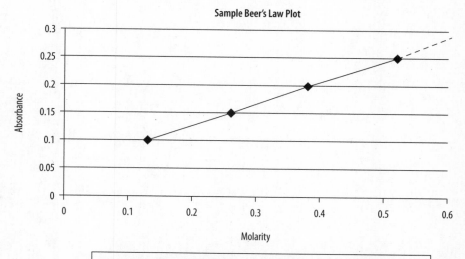

Beer's law says that absorbance of a molecule or solution is:
Absorbance (A) = (a)(b)(c)

▸ a is the absorptivity (measured by amount of light absorbed by 1 cm of a 1 M solution)

▸ b is the path length (in units of centimeters, cm)

▸ c is the concentration (in units of molar, M)

Absorbance is linearly proportional to the thickness of the sample, the concentration of the absorbing medium, and the absorptivity, which is a measure of a given molecule's ability to absorb light.

Sample Beer's Law Plot

Extrapolation of the curve (dotted lines) shows that an absorbance of 0.30 reflects a 0.6M solution.

Free-Response Writing

Part I. The Periodic Table

The free-response section will contain a standard periodic table that has the atomic number, the element abbreviation and the atomic mass with either 1 or 2 decimal places (part I of the test will also have a periodic table). An example of such is below.

26
Fe
55.85

Part II. The Reference Sheet(s)

There are three pages of reference material that are located in the free-response section. At first glance this section can be quite intimidating for students because of the many formulas, constants, and standard reduction potentials included. The truth of the matter is the reference section is there so that students across the country are all on an equal playing field. The most helpful thing you can do for yourself is to download the most recent free-response questions for the AP Chemistry exam from the College Board's AP Central website (*http://apcentral.collegeboard.com*). These questions contain the reference guides that will be on your test. The reference section is broken up into topics which makes it easy to find the information you may need. Check the equations that you know and use them to cross-reference the chapters in this book. You will quickly see that you already know many of the formulas and that there is no need to panic.

Part III. Being Neat for the Reader

AP readers are inclined to give the neat student the benefit of the doubt when grading the free-response questions. You do not want the reader to have to look too hard for your answer. To be neat, do the following:

1. The AP questions will have multiple parts to them labeled with letters. You should write the letter in parentheses and answer the question in the space provided.
2. Use the bullet technique after each lettered question. Bullet your calculation or explanation so the reader can find it and not have to search the entire page.
3. Drawing a diagram is a great way to show the reader that you know your stuff. Every accurate drawing should be followed with a short explanation so the reader can give you full credit for the question.
4. As stated in Chapter 22, "Communication of Results," use factor label, significant figures, and circle your final numerical answer for the reader.

Part IV. Be Brief But Articulate

Unlike some other AP exams, such as AP Biology, you do not have to write a lot for the AP Chemistry exam. Limit your explanations to one or two sentences. Several key phrases and words that are common to look for include these:

1. CALCULATE means you need to provide a numerical answer to the question.
2. WRITE THE FORMULA means you need to provide the reader with an accurate chemical formula that relates to the question.